Thomism and the Problem of Animal Suffering

Thomism and the Problem of Animal Suffering

B. Kyle Keltz

WIPF & STOCK · Eugene, Oregon

THOMISM AND THE PROBLEM OF ANIMAL SUFFERING

Copyright © 2020 B. Kyle Keltz. All rights reserved. Except for brief quotations in critical publications or reviews, no part of this book may be reproduced in any manner without prior written permission from the publisher. Write: Permissions, Wipf and Stock Publishers, 199 W. 8th Ave., Suite 3, Eugene, OR 97401.

Wipf & Stock
An Imprint of Wipf and Stock Publishers
199 W. 8th Ave., Suite 3
Eugene, OR 97401

www.wipfandstock.com

PAPERBACK ISBN: 978-1-7252-7280-4
HARDCOVER ISBN: 978-1-7252-7279-8
EBOOK ISBN: 978-1-7252-7281-1

Manufactured in the U.S.A.   06/10/20

Scripture quotations taken from the New American Standard Bible® (NASB), Copyright © 1960, 1962, 1963, 1968, 1971, 1972, 1973, 1975, 1977, 1995 by The Lockman Foundation Used by permission. www.Lockman.org

Contents

Abbreviations | vii

1. The Problem of Animal Suffering | 1
2. The Nature of Animal Suffering and God's Goodness | 34
3. The Nature of the Animal Soul | 60
4. Animal Suffering and God's Purpose for the Universe | 89
5. Could a Good God Allow Death before the Fall? | 111

Appendix: A Thomistic Answer to the Evil-God Challenge | 133
Bibliography | 145
Index | 155

Abbreviations

De anima	Thomas Aquinas. *Quaestiones disputatae de anima*. Translation available in Robb, James H., trans. *Questions on the Soul*. Milwaukee: Marquette University Press, 1984.
De Ente	Thomas Aquinas. *De ente et essentia*. Translation available in Maurer, Armand, trans. *On Being and Essence*. 2nd rev. ed. Toronto: Pontifical Institue of Mediaeval Studies, 1968.
De Malo	Thomas Aquinas. *Quaestiones disputatae de malo*. In *On Evil*. Translated by Richard Regan. Edited by Brian Davies. New York: Oxford University Press, 2003.
De Veritate	Thomas Aquinas. *Quaestiones disputatae de veritate*. Translation available in Mulligan, Robert W., et al., trans. *Truth*. 3 vols. Indianapolis: Hackett, 1994.
In De Anima	Thomas Aquinas. *Sentencia libri De anima*. In *Aristotle's De Anima with the Commentary of St. Thomas Aquinas*. Translated by Kenelm Foster and Sylvester Humphries. New Haven: Yale University Press, 1951.
SCG	Thomas Aquinas. *Summa contra Gentiles*. In *Summa Contra Gentiles*. Translated by Laurence Shapcote. Aquinas Institute, Inc. https://aquinas.cc/la/en/~SCG1.
ST	Thomas Aquinas. *Summa theologiae*. In *Summa Theologiae*. Edited by John Mortensen and Enrique Alarcón. Translated by Laurence Shapcote. Aquinas Institute, Inc. https://aquinas.cc/la/en/~ST.I.

1

The Problem of Animal Suffering

THE PROBLEM OF EVIL is an issue that humans have pondered since ancient times.[1] "Why do people suffer and die, and why do people mistreat each other so much?" In the context of theism, the problem of evil becomes even worse. It is assumed that if there is an all-good, all-powerful, and all-knowing God who created and sustains the world, then that God would prevent evil from happening; yet evil occurs each day in our world.

Of course, there are many proposed solutions to the problem. Many theists (at least as far back as Augustine of Hippo[2]) have argued that people are allowed to perform evil because God wants a world with free-willed beings.[3] The only way for God to guarantee that no evil occur would be for him to eliminate the free will of angels and humans. But for various reasons, God wants a world with free-willed beings. Thus, God allows evil by preserving free will. Moral evil (e.g., theft, murder, rape, etc.) exists because humans have free will, and natural evil (e.g., disease, earthquakes, tornadoes, death, etc.) possibly exists because of the free will of fallen angels.[4]

Other theists (at least as far back as Irenaeus[5]) have argued that God allows evil so humans will mature spiritually in preparation for living with

---

1. In Western philosophy, discussions of the problem of evil go as far back as Plato's *Republic* (2.379b) and *Timaeus* (e.g., 29e and 30b). See Hickson, "Brief History of Problems of Evil," 4–6.

2. For examples, see Augustine, *Lib.* 2.17; and Augustine, *Enchir.* 8.23. See also Augustine, *Civ.* 12–14.

3. See van Woudenberg, "Brief History of Theodicy," 179–81, 184–85, 187–88; and Speak, "Free Will and Soul-Making Theodicies," 205–21.

4. See Dunnington, "Problem with the Satan Hypothesis," 265–74.

5. See Irenaeus, *Epid.* 12.

God forever in the afterlife.[6] If moral evil did not exist, humans would never learn the value of moral choices. Moreover, without natural evil, humans would not fully appreciate living with God in an afterlife devoid of suffering. This soul-making view concludes that the existence of evil is not an accident because it is intended for a good purpose.

The history of Christian philosophy is filled with discussions on evil and why God might allow it. Yet, the discussion, until recent times, has focused on why bad things are allowed to happen to human beings. Theists generally did not think it necessary to provide a reason for why God allows nonhuman animals to suffer and die. Until modern times, theists believed that animals were created by God specifically to serve and provide food for humans.[7] Christian theologians, such as Augustine, argued that predatory animals were necessary for the beauty of the world.[8] Following Aristotle, Thomas Aquinas did not believe that nonhuman animal suffering is morally significant because nonhuman animals do not possess rational souls.[9]

It seems that two main factors gave rise to a higher awareness of animal suffering among Christian theologians in the modern period: social changes and scientific advancements. Regarding social changes, pet-keeping became widespread in Europe among the middle class in the 1600s.[10] Derek Wiertel believes that although pet-keeping was not new to European society, especially among the upper classes, pet-keeping was a crucial factor in "deepening" an appreciation for the moral status of nonhuman animals.[11]

Scientists increasingly began uncovering evidence for the vast amount of nonhuman animal suffering in this period also. In the late 1600s, English natural philosopher Robert Hooke confirmed that fossils were the preserved remains of once-living organisms (*Micrographia*, 1665). In the late 1700s, scientists, such as Comte de Buffon (*Les Époques de la Nature*, 1778) and Pierre Laplace (*Exposition du système du monde*, 1796), theorized that the earth was formed according to natural laws over a long period of time. In the 1800s, Jean Lamarck proposed the idea that animals can acquire new traits

---

6. See van Woudenberg, "Brief History of Theodicy," 178; and Speak, "Free Will and Soul-Making Theodicies," 205–21.

7. For a detailed discussion of the factors giving rise to awareness of the tension between theism and animal suffering, see Wiertel, "Classical Theism and the Problem of Animal Suffering," 669–72.

8. Augustine, *Gen. litt.* 3.16, 25.

9. This will be discussed in more detail in chapter 3.

10. Wiertel, "Classical Theism and the Problem of Animal Suffering," 670.

11. Wiertel, "Classical Theism and the Problem of Animal Suffering," 670.

based on the environment in which they live (*Philosophie Zoologique*, 1809), and Charles Darwin theorized that animal populations arise from common descent and natural selection (*On the Origin of Species*, 1859).

As more scientists concluded that the earth and all life on earth formed through natural processes over long periods of time, so also did they become increasingly aware of the vast amount of nonhuman animal suffering in the earth's natural history. Among these scientists, Darwin's comments on nonhuman animal suffering are probably the most famous. In a letter to Asa Gray on May 22, 1860, Darwin wrote,

> With respect to the theological view of the question; this is always painful to me. I am bewildered. I had no intention to write atheistically. But I own that I cannot see, as plainly as others do, & as I should wish to do, evidence of design & beneficence on all sides of us. There seems to me too much misery in the world. I cannot persuade myself that a beneficent & omnipotent God would have designedly created the Ichneumonidæ with the express intention of their feeding within the living bodies of caterpillars, or that a cat should play with mice. Not believing this, I see no necessity in the belief that the eye was expressly designed. On the other hand I cannot anyhow be contented to view this wonderful universe & especially the nature of man, & to conclude that everything is the result of brute force. I am inclined to look at everything as resulting from designed laws, with the details, whether good or bad, left to the working out of what we may call chance. Not that this notion *at all* satisfies me. I feel most deeply that the whole subject is too profound for the human intellect. A dog might as well speculate on the mind of Newton. Let each man hope & believe what he can.[12]

As is apparent, Darwin struggled with the understanding that a sovereign, all-good, all-powerful, and all-knowing God sustains a world in which nonhuman animals have been and are preyed upon by each other. Specifically, it seemed to Darwin that God would not intentionally design and create parasitoids like the Ichneumonidae, which reproduce by injecting their eggs into the bodies of their prey.

The tension that arises between the awareness of animal suffering and theism is known today as the *problem of animal suffering*. Basically, the problem involves the question of the reconciliation of the concepts of an all-good, all-knowing, all-powerful God and a world that contains a

---

12. Darwin, "Letter no. 2814," para. 3 (emphasis in original).

vast amount of nonhuman animal suffering. Proponents of the problem of animal suffering argue that the God of theism most likely does not exist because such a God would not use millions of years of animal pain, disease, suffering, and death to create a world meant for humans. This chapter will provide an introduction to the problem of animal suffering by surveying major figures in the history of the problem and then discussing the current status of the debate over the problem.

Proponents of the Problem of Animal Suffering

Today, theists are trying to answer two main formulations of the problem of animal suffering from William Rowe and Paul Draper. However, there have been several proponents of the problem through the years in addition to Rowe and Draper. Prominent proponents of the problem include David Hume, Charles Darwin, John Fiske, Bertrand Russell, Quentin Smith, David L. Hull, and Richard Dawkins.

In addition to the above quote, Darwin is also famous for at least two other sayings in regard to the problem of animal suffering. In a letter to Joseph Hooker in 1856, while discussing nonhuman animal hermaphrodites, Darwin wrote, "What a book a Devil's chaplain might write on the clumsy, wasteful, blundering low and horridly cruel works of nature!"[13] Toward the end of his life, in 1876, Darwin wrote in his autobiography what is probably his most clear statement of the problem of animal suffering:

> That there is much suffering in the world no one disputes. Some have attempted to explain this in reference to man by imagining that it serves for his moral improvement. But the number of men in the world is as nothing compared with that of all other sentient beings, and these often suffer greatly without any moral improvement. A being so powerful and so full of knowledge as a God who would create the universe, is to our finite minds omnipotent and omniscient, and it revolts our understanding to suppose that his benevolence is not unbounded, for what advantage can there be in the sufferings of millions of the lower animals throughout almost endless time? This very old argument from the existence of suffering against the existence of an intelligent first cause seems to me a strong one; whereas, as just remarked, the presence of much

---

13. Darwin, "Letter no. 1924," para. 1.

suffering agrees well with the view that all organic beings have been developed through variation and Natural Selection.[14]

Darwin here is saying he finds arguments against theism compelling based on the amount of animal suffering found in the natural history of the earth, and these arguments are compatible with his theory of natural selection.

It is not clear as to which "very old argument" Darwin is referring because, as mentioned, the problem of animal suffering mainly arose in the modern era. However, Darwin is possibly referring to an argument found in the writings of David Hume.[15] In *Dialogues Concerning Natural Religion*, Hume's character Philo argues,

> Is the world, considered in general, and as it appears to us in this life, different from what a man or such a limited being would, *beforehand*, expect from a very powerful, wise, and benevolent deity? It must be strange prejudice to assert the contrary. And from thence I conclude, that, however consistent the world may be, allowing certain suppositions and conjectures, with the idea of such a deity, it can never afford us an inference concerning his existence. The consistency is not absolutely denied, only the inference.... There seem to be *four* circumstances, on which depend all, or the greatest part of the ills, that molest sensible creatures; and it is not impossible but all these circumstances may be necessary and unavoidable.... The *first* circumstance, which introduces evil, is that contrivance or economy of the animal creation, by which pains, as well as pleasures, are employed to excite all creatures to action, and make them vigilant in the great work of self-preservation. Now pleasure alone, in its various degrees, seems to human understanding sufficient for this purpose. All animals might be constantly in a state of enjoyment; but when urged by any of the necessities of nature, such as thirst, hunger, weariness; instead of pain, they might feel a diminution of pleasure, by which they might be prompted to seek that object, which is necessary to their subsistence. Men pursue pleasure as eagerly as they avoid pain; at least, might have been so constituted. It seems, therefore, plainly possible to carry on the business of life without any pain. Why then is any animal ever rendered susceptible of such a sensation? If animals can be free from it an hour, they might enjoy a perpetual exemption from it; and it required as particular a contrivance of their organs to produce that feeling,

---

14. Darwin, *Autobiography of Charles Darwin*, 121–22.

15. It is known that Darwin was influenced by Hume's thought in several areas. For example, see Huntley, "David Hume and Charles Darwin," 457–70.

> as to endow them with sight, hearing, or any of the senses. Shall we conjecture, that such a contrivance was necessary, without any appearances of reason? And shall we build on that conjecture as on the most certain truth?[16]

Philo is arguing that the ability to feel pain is not something that someone would expect from an all-knowing, all-powerful, and all-good God to create. It does not seem absolutely necessary for nonhuman animals and humans to be able to feel pain. If the God of theism created the world, it seems possible that he could have done so without including pain. Philo suggests that the withdrawal of pleasure could serve the same function as the experience of pain in motiving organisms to avoid harm. Since humans pursue pleasure as much as they seek to avoid pain, it seems reasonable, as the argument goes, to conclude that pain is unnecessary.

John Fiske, an American historian and philosopher, was a contemporary of Darwin and was greatly impressed by the philosophical import of Darwin's evolutionary theory. Fiske was introduced to evolutionary thought through the writings of Herbert Spencer, whose teachings on evolutionary theory strongly influenced Fiske.[17] Fiske incorporated evolutionary theory in his writings and attempted to apply it to his theories on the development of human history and social institutions. In one such work, in regard to whether God used evolution to form the world as it currently was, Fiske wrote,

> Just so far as the correspondence between the organism and its environment is complete, does the teleological hypothesis find apparent confirmation. Just so far as the correspondence is incomplete, does it meet with patent contradiction. If harmony and fitness are to be cited as proofs of beneficent design, then discord and unfitness must equally be kept in view as evidences of less admirable contrivance. A scheme which permits thousands of generations to live and die in wretchedness, cannot, merely by providing for the well-being of later ages, be absolved from the alternative charge of awkwardness or malevolence. If there exist a personal Creator of the universe who is infinitely intelligent and powerful, he cannot be infinitely good: if, on the other hand, he be infinite in goodness, then he must be lamentably finite in power or in intelligence. By this two-edged difficulty, Theology has ever been foiled.[18]

---

16. Hume, *Dialogues Concerning Natural Religion*, 11.205–6 (emphasis in original).
17. Clark, *Life and Letters of John Fiske*, 293–95.
18. Fiske, *Outlines of Cosmic Philosophy*, 405.

The Problem of Animal Suffering

Here Fiske is arguing that if God specially created the world, then God's goodness or power and knowledge are questionable. If God is all-good, all-powerful, and all-knowing and created the world without using natural selection, it would seem that animals would always be fit for their environment and never face extinction. Yet, the natural history of the earth shows that many generations of animals have faced environments for which they were not suited, and they passed away, leaving only the best of their kind.

For Fiske, animal suffering deemed it necessary to cast out anthropomorphic attributes, such as moral goodness, from the concept of God:

> I will add that it is impossible to call that Being good, who, existing prior to the phenomenal universe, and creating it out of the plenitude of infinite power and foreknowledge, endowed it with such properties that its material and moral development must inevitably be attended by the misery of untold millions of sentient creatures for whose existence their Creator is ultimately alone responsible. *In short, there can be no hypothesis, of a "moral government" of the world, which does not implicitly assert an immoral government.* As soon as we seek to go beyond the process of evolution disclosed by science, and posit an external Agency which is in the slightest degree anthropomorphic, we are obliged either to supplement and limit this Agency by a second one that is diabolic, or else to include elements of diabolism in the character of the first Agency itself.[19]

Thus, according to Fiske, in light of animal suffering, if God is personal, God cannot be all-good unless he is lacking in knowledge or power or both.

In contemporary times, philosopher and logician Bertrand Russell commented on the problem of animal suffering in his writings on science and religion. Russell's oft-quoted passage summarizes the problem well:

> Religion, in our day, has accommodated itself to the doctrine of evolution, and has even derived new arguments from it. We are told that "through the ages one increasing purpose runs," and that evolution is the unfolding of an idea which has been in the mind of God throughout. It appears that during those ages which so troubled Hugh Miller, when animals were torturing each other with ferocious horns and agonizing stings, Omnipotence was quietly waiting for the ultimate emergence of man, with his still more exquisite powers of torture and his far more widely diffused cruelty. Why the Creator should have preferred to reach His goal by a process, instead of going straight to it, these modern theologians

---

19. Fiske, *Outlines of Cosmic Philosophy*, 407 (emphasis in original).

do not tell us. Nor do they say much to allay our doubts as to the gloriousness of the consummation. It is difficult not to feel, as the boy did after being taught the alphabet, that it was not worth going through so much to get so little.[20]

As Russell emphasizes, it seems counterintuitive that God would use millions of years of nonhuman animal suffering with the sole intention of creating a home for humanity.

Atheist philosopher Quentin Smith has argued that the God of theism cannot exist because of the existence of "evil natural laws." He explains,

> Not long ago I was sleeping in a cabin in the woods and was awoken in the middle of the night by the sounds of a struggle between two animals. Cries of terror and extreme agony rent the night, intermingled with the sounds of jaws snapping bones and flesh being torn from limbs. One animal was being savagely attacked, killed and then devoured by another.
>
> A clearer case of a horrible event in nature, a natural evil, has never been presented to me. It seemed to me self-evident that the natural law that *animals must savagely kill and devour each other in order to survive* was an evil natural law and that the obtaining of this law was sufficient that God did not exist.[21]

Based on this experience, Smith formulates a "probabilistic" argument against the existence of God:

(1) God is omnipotent, omniscient, and omnibenevolent.

(2) If God exists, then there exist no instances of an ultimately evil natural law.

(3) It is probable that the law of predation is ultimately evil.

(4) It is probable that there exist instances of the law of predation.

Therefore, it is probable that

(5) God does not exist.[22]

Smith defends premise (3) of his argument on the basis that it is possible that God could have made a world with the same animals yet without carnivorous natures. In other words, God could have made a world with lions

---

20. Russell, *Religion and Science*, 79–80.
21. Smith, "Atheological Argument from Evil Natural Laws," 159 (emphasis in original).
22. Smith, "Atheological Argument from Evil Natural Laws," 160.

The Problem of Animal Suffering

that are herbivores. Such a world, Smith argues, would be better or at least equivalent to this world but without the violence that goes with animals devouring each other. Even if a natural law that includes animal predation is meant for the good of carnivores and their surrounding environments, it is ultimately evil because it could have been avoided by simply making a world with the herbivore equivalents of each kind of carnivore. However, since our world contains natural processes that entail predation, it is probable that God does not exist.

Philosopher of science David L. Hull is noted for his comments regarding the problem of animal suffering. Hull is mainly known for his work that established the contemporary field of the philosophy of biology. However, in a review of Phillip E. Johnson's *Darwin on Trial*, Hull argues,

> The problem that biological evolution poses for natural theologians is the sort of God that a darwinian version of evolution implies.
>
> What kind of God can one infer from the sort of phenomena epitomized by the species on Darwin's Galápagos Islands? The evolutionary process is rife with happenstance, contingency, incredible waste, death, pain and horror. . . . When the eggs that cuckoos lay in the nests of other birds hatch, the cuckoo chick proceeds to push the eggs of its foster parents out of the nest. The queens of a particular species of parasitic ant have only one remarkable adaptation, a serrated appendage which they use to saw off the head of the host queen. . . .
>
> Whatever the God implied by evolutionary theory and the data of natural history may be like, He is not the Protestant God of waste not, want not. He is also not a loving God who cares about His productions. He is not even the awful God portrayed in the book of Job. The God of the Galápagos is careless, wasteful, indifferent, almost diabolical. He is certainly not the sort of God to whom anyone would be inclined to pray.[23]

To Hull, an all-good, all-knowing, all-powerful God would not create a world in which animals survive by killing other animals or a world in which living things are not suited for their environments. The God of the Bible would create a world without waste, death, or pain. Thus, the God of the Bible must not exist, and all that is left, if anything, is the "God of the Galápagos."

Finally, evolutionary biologist Richard Dawkins is no stranger to publicly attacking Christianity, theism, and religion in general. In his popular science book, *A River out of Eden*, Dawkins argues,

23. Hull, "God of the Galápagos," 486.

> So long as DNA is passed on, it does not matter who or what gets hurt in the process. It is better for the genes of Darwin's ichneumon wasp that the caterpillar should be alive, and therefore fresh, when it is eaten, no matter what the cost in suffering. Genes don't care about suffering, because they don't care about anything.
>
> If Nature were kind, she would at least make the minor concession of anesthetizing caterpillars before they are eaten alive from within. But Nature is neither kind nor unkind. She is neither against suffering nor for it. Nature is not interested one way or the other in suffering, unless it affects the survival of DNA. It is easy to imagine a gene that, say, tranquilizes gazelles when they are about to suffer a killing bite. Would such a gene be favored by natural selection? Not unless the act of tranquilizing a gazelle improved that gene's chances of being propagated into future generations. It is hard to see why this should be so, and we may therefore guess that gazelles suffer horrible pain and fear when they are pursued to the death—as most of them eventually are. The total amount of suffering per year in the natural world is beyond all decent contemplation. During the minute it takes me to compose this sentence, thousands of animals are being eaten alive; others are running for their lives, whimpering with fear; others are being slowly devoured from within by rasping parasites; thousands of all kinds are dying of starvation, thirst and disease. It must be so. If there is ever a time of plenty, this very fact will automatically lead to an increase in population until the natural state of starvation and misery is restored....
>
> In a universe of blind physical forces and genetic replication, some people are going to get hurt, other people are going to get lucky, and you won't find any rhyme or reason in it, nor any justice. The universe we observe has precisely the properties we should expect if there is, at bottom, no design, no purpose, no evil and no good, nothing but blind, pitiless indifference.[24]

Dawkins is saying that, given the world we observe, especially noting the amount of nonhuman animal suffering that occurs daily, it is more reasonable to believe that there is no God. If an all-powerful, all-knowing, and all-good God created the world for a purpose, we would expect much less (if any) suffering. There should not be any suffering, or we should at least find genes that anesthetize nonhuman animals before they are eaten and other similar genetic traits that would make life easier and less horrifying for nonhuman animals.

24. Dawkins, *River out of Eden*, 131–33.

The Problem of Animal Suffering

William L. Rowe

Out of all the arguments that will be covered in this book, the one that has been discussed the most in the philosophy of religion originated with William Rowe. His argument has not always been discussed in the context of the problem of animal suffering. However, it is most certainly relevant.

In "The Problem of Evil and Some Varieties of Atheism," Rowe's purpose was to formulate an argument concluding that it is reasonable to be an atheist. This distinguished his argument from other formulations of the problem of evil (such as J. L. Mackie's[25]) in that his argument was not meant to show that theism is incoherent but that theism is most likely false. He begins,

> In developing the argument for atheism based on the existence of evil, it will be useful to focus on some particular evil that our world contains in considerable abundance. Intense human and animal suffering, for example, occurs daily and in great plenitude in our world. Such intense suffering is a clear case of evil.[26]

Rowe mentions that the human and nonhuman animal suffering in the world is a "clear case of evil." This leads to his famous fawn-in-the-woods example. He says to

> Suppose in some distant forest lightning strikes a dead tree, resulting in a forest fire. In the fire a fawn is trapped, horribly burned, and lies in terrible agony for several days before death relieves its suffering.[27]

Rowe provides this as an example of what is now commonly referred to as a "gratuitous evil" or a "pointless evil." He says,

> So far as we can see, the fawn's intense suffering is pointless. For there does not appear to be any greater good such that the prevention of the fawn's suffering would require either the loss of that good or the occurrence of an evil equally bad or worse. Nor does there seem to be an equally bad or worse evil so connected to the fawn's suffering that it would have had to occur had the fawn's suffering been prevented.[28]

---

25. Mackie, "Evil and Omnipotence," 200–212.
26. Rowe, "Problem of Evil and Some Varieties of Atheism," 335.
27. Rowe, "Problem of Evil and Some Varieties of Atheism," 337.
28. Rowe, "Problem of Evil and Some Varieties of Atheism," 337.

Given this example of nonhuman animal suffering and his concept of pointless suffering, Rowe formulated what is now known as an evidential problem of evil:

1. There exist instances of intense suffering which an omnipotent, omniscient being could have prevented without thereby losing some greater good or permitting some evil equally bad or worse.

2. An omniscient, wholly good being would prevent the occurrence of any intense suffering it could, unless it could not do so without thereby losing some greater good or permitting some evil equally bad or worse.

3. There does not exist an omnipotent, omniscient, wholly good being.[29]

After presenting this argument, Rowe emphasizes that while it is uncertain whether any cases of animal suffering are pointless, it is rational to assume that at least some are pointless, given the great amount that occur in the world.[30] This is said to be an evidential problem because the great amount of suffering increases the probability of this argument being true. There are so many cases of intense suffering that it is believed to be rational to conclude that some of these instances of suffering are pointless (although it is difficult, if not impossible, to know if there is a good reason for each case of intense suffering in the world).

Paul Draper

Several versions of the evidential problem of evil based in nonhuman animal pain and suffering have been proposed by Paul Draper.[31] Draper does not propose an inductive argument against theism like Rowe, but instead, following Darwin, often argues that the great amount of nonhuman animal

---

29. Rowe, "Problem of Evil and Some Varieties of Atheism," 336.

30. "The truth is that we are not in a position to prove that (1) is true. We cannot know with certainty that instances of suffering of the sort described in (1) do occur in our world. But it is one thing to know or prove that (1) is true and quite another thing to have rational grounds for believing (1) to be true" (Rowe, "Problem of Evil and Some Varieties of Atheism," 337).

31. See Draper, "Pain and Pleasure: An Evidential Problem for Theists," 331–50; Draper, "Cosmic Fine-Tuning and Terrestrial Suffering," 311–21; Draper, "Darwin's Argument from Evil," 49–70; Draper, "Christian Theism and Life on Earth," 306–16; and Draper, "Evolution and the Problem of Evil," 271–82.

death and floundering can be better explained by indifferent naturalism rather than Christian theism.[32]

One pertinent argument of Draper's is found in his essay titled "Darwin's Argument from Evil." Draper says the theory of natural selection

> can serve as a good 'atheodicy': an explanation of various facts about good and evil that works much better on the assumption that an alternative to theism—in this case the no-design hypothesis—is true than on the assumption that orthodox theism is true.[33]

Here he is attempting to formulate an argument that is a philosophically rigorous extension of Darwin's comments regarding animal suffering. In one of three arguments (which are derived from the writings of Charles Darwin), Draper says, "Darwinian explanations of good and evil are less complete when Darwin's theory is combined with theism than when it is combined with the no-design hypothesis."[34] Draper argues that the truth of evolutionary theory provides evidence for naturalism rather than theism because "Darwin's theory comes closer to solving the puzzle of good and evil faced by the proponent of the no-design hypothesis than the puzzle of good and evil faced by the theist."[35] In other words, the existence of good and evil will never be explained because "any complete explanation of facts about good and evil, if theism is true, include God's moral justification for allowing those facts to obtain."[36] Given God's hiddenness, we may never know why he allows evil in most situations. So, if theism is true, then we may never be able to explain facts about good and evil. However, evolutionary theory does explain the occurrence of good and evil, assuming the truth of the no-design hypothesis.

Another pertinent argument comes from Draper's essay titled "Christian Theism and Life on Earth." In this essay, Draper's thesis includes the argument that the specific amount of "flourishing and floundering" of sentient organisms on earth provides evidence for naturalism over theism. He emphasizes,

> What we find when we examine our biosphere is that, for a variety of biological and ecological reasons, organisms compete for

---

32. Draper, "Christian Theism and Life on Earth," 306–16.
33. Draper, "Darwin's Argument from Evil," 58.
34. Draper, "Darwin's Argument from Evil," 63.
35. Draper, "Darwin's Argument from Evil," 65.
36. Draper, "Darwin's Argument from Evil," 65.

survival, with some having an advantage in the struggle for survival over others; as a result, many organisms, including many sentient beings, never flourish because they die before maturity, many others barely survive, but languish for most or all of their lives, and those that reach maturity and flourish for much of their lives usually flounder in old age; further, in the case of human beings and very probably some non-human animals as well, floundering or languishing often involves intense and prolonged suffering.[37]

Given that the God of Christianity should want his creatures to flourish and has the power to make this so, Draper concludes that "the fact that huge numbers of human and other sentient beings never flourish at all before death and countless others flourish only briefly, is extremely surprising given CT [Christian theism]. It is not what one would expect to find in a living world created by the Christian God."[38]

As mentioned, the arguments of Rowe and Draper are discussed the most in the literature regarding the problem of animal suffering. While many have discussed the tension between the God of theism and the apparent amount of nonhuman animal suffering in nature, no one developed the problem to the extent of Rowe and Draper. As such, in this book, I will be concerned mainly with their arguments, although I will occasionally mention the arguments of the other proponents of the problem of animal suffering.

Opponents of the Problem of Animal Suffering

Again, the problem of animal suffering did not emerge and was not considered a major problem for theism until modern times. Yet in the Western philosophical tradition, the belief that nonhuman animals are drastically different from humans is found at least as far back as Aristotle.

Aristotle postulated three main types of souls in nature: vegetative, sensitive, and rational souls.[39] He believed the soul is not only the principle of life in an organism but also that which makes possible different abilities across the three kinds of souls. The vegetative soul is the form of organisms such as plants. Organisms with vegetative souls are able to process nutrients, grow and develop, and reproduce themselves. The soul of an animal is a sensitive soul. Included in sensitive souls are the abilities of movement

---

37. Draper, "Christian Theism and Life on Earth," 312.
38. Draper, "Christian Theism and Life on Earth," 313.
39. Aristotle, *De an.* 2.3.

and sensation in addition to the abilities of vegetative souls. The soul of human beings is the rational soul. Like the sensitive soul, the rational soul includes the abilities of the souls beneath it. However, the rational soul has the unique abilities of the intellect and will. This belief that nonhuman animals lack rational souls is a major factor in Aristotle's view of the *telos* of nonhuman animals:

> Property, of this sort, then, is evidently given by nature itself to all living things straight from when they are first conceived, and similarly too when they have reached completion. And in fact some animals produce at the start, together with their offspring, enough food to last the latter until such time as it is able to get it for itself—for example, those that produce grubs or eggs. Animals that give birth to live offspring, on the other hand, carry food for their offspring in their own bodies for a certain period—namely, the natural substance called milk. It is clear, then, in the case of developed things too, that we must suppose both that plants are for the sake of animals, and that the other animals are for the sake of humans, domestic ones both for using and eating, and if not at all, nonetheless most, wild ones for food and other sorts of support, so that clothes and other instruments may be got from them. If then nature makes nothing incomplete and nothing pointlessly, it must be that nature made all of them for the sake of humans.[40]

Nature does not make incomplete or useless things, and just as plants are meant to feed nonhuman animals, so also are nonhuman animals meant to serve and provide food for humans.

Augustine and Aquinas

Medieval theists generally followed Aristotle in thinking that nonhuman animals lack rationality and exist to provide humans with food, clothing, free labor, etc. When writing on nonhuman animals, they most often did so in the context of the question of the moral status of nonhuman animals. Among medieval theologians, Augustine and Aquinas are two prominent examples of theists who wrote about nonhuman animals.

---

40. Aristotle, *Pol.* 1.8.

Augustine believed in a similar hierarchy as that of Aristotle, albeit a Christian hierarchy that spanned from inanimate objects to angels.[41] Augustine explains,

> Among all things which somehow exist and which can be distinguished from God who made them, those that live are ranked higher than those that do not, that is to say, those that have the power of reproduction or even of appetite are above those which lack this faculty. In that order of living things, the sentient are superior to the non-sentient, for example, animals to trees. Among sentient beings, the intelligent are higher than the non-intelligent, as with men and cattle. Among the intelligent, the immortal are superior to the mortal, as angels to men.
>
> This is the hierarchy according to the order of nature.[42]

Augustine's understanding that nonhuman animals are arational entails that nonhuman animals are unable to sin and that they have no moral standing.[43] In this regard, when commenting on the morality of suicide and the biblical command to refrain from killing, Augustine mentions,

> Must we, then, when we read, 'Thou shalt not kill,' understand that it is a crime to pull up a shrub, and foolishly subscribe to the error of the Manichaeans?
>
> Putting this nonsense aside, we do not apply 'Thou shalt not kill' to plants, because they have no sensation; or to irrational animals that fly, swim, walk, or creep, because they are linked to us by no association or common bond. By the Creator's wise ordinance they are meant for our use, dead or alive. It only remains for us to apply the commandment 'Thou shalt not kill,' to man alone, oneself and others. And, of course, one who kills himself kills a man.[44]

Aquinas held a similar view to Augustine. In keeping with his integration of Aristotle's philosophy into his Christian philosophy, Aquinas held that nonhuman animals lack the rational soul that humans possess.[45] He argues that God created a hierarchy of beings to communicate God's goodness and that the lower beings in the hierarchy (i.e., plants and nonhuman

---

41. For a detailed overview of Augustine on the moral status of nonhuman animals, see Steiner, *Anthropocentrism and Its Discontents*, 116–19.

42. Augustine, *Civ.* 11.16.

43. See Augustine, *Gen. litt.* 3.16, 25.

44. Augustine, *Civ.* 1.20.

45. See *ST* II-II, q. 25, a. 3.

animals) exist for the good of the beings above them (i.e., humans).[46] For example, he concludes,

> Hereby is refuted the error of those who said it is sinful for a man to kill dumb animals: for by divine providence they are intended for man's use in the natural order. Hence it is no wrong for man to make use of them, either by killing or in any other way whatever. For this reason the Lord said to Noah: *As I gave you the green plants, I have delivered all flesh to you* (Gen 9:3).[47]

Augustine and Aquinas do not mention the problem of animal suffering because they both believed that nonhuman animals are arational and were created by God to serve, feed, and clothe humans.

René Descartes

Although Augustine and Aquinas are usually mentioned with disdain by animal advocates, probably the most infamous Christian philosopher regarding the debate over the moral status of nonhuman animals is René Descartes. This is because Descartes is often credited with the idea that nonhuman animals are like machines in that they are completely devoid of sentience.[48] Peter Harrison explains,

> The father of modern philosophy is credited with the opinion that animals are non-sentient automata, an opinion for which over the centuries he has been ridiculed and vilified. It [Descartes's view of animals] has been variously characterized as 'an internecine and murderous view', a 'monstrous thesis', an 'irredeemably fatuous belief', a doctrine which 'brutally violates the old kindly fellowship of living things.'[49]

Indeed, many of Descartes's writings lend support to the interpretation that nonhuman animals lack sentience, and his philosophical dualism easily leads to this conclusion.[50]

---

46. *SCG* II, c. 45; III, c. 112.
47. *SCG* III, c. 112.
48. Harrison, "Descartes on Animals," 219.
49. Harrison, "Descartes on Animals," 219. See More, "More to Descartes, 11 December 1648," 5:243; Smith, *New Studies in the Philosophy of Descartes*, 135–36; Clark, *Moral Status of Animals*, 37; and Gibson, *Philosophy of Descartes*, 214, respectively, for the quotes that Harrison provides.
50. Harrison, "Descartes on Animals," 222.

Thomism and the Problem of Animal Suffering

Descartes believed that humans are comprised of a physical body and a mind or soul that is immaterial. His philosophy entails that the body is a distinct physical substance, and the soul is a distinct spiritual substance.[51] The mind/soul is what thinks, feels, etc. and, according to the popular interpretation of Descartes, also that which causes consciousness.[52] For example, in *Meditations on First Philosophy*, Descartes seems to include conscious feeling as a function of the human mind/soul and says feelings are the same as thoughts:

> But what then am I? A thing which thinks. What is a thing which thinks? It is a thing which doubts, understands, [conceives], affirms, denies, wills, refuses, which also imagines and *feels*. . . .
>
> For it is so evident of itself that it is I who doubts, who understands, and who desires, that there is no reason here to add anything to explain it. And I have certainly the power of imagining likewise; for although it may happen (as I formerly supposed) that none of the things which I imagine are true, nevertheless this power of imagining does not cease to be really in use, and it forms part of my thought.
>
> Finally, I am the same who *feels*, that is to say, who *perceives certain things*, as by the organs of sense, since in truth I see light, I hear noise, I feel heat. But it will be said that these phenomena are false and that I am dreaming. Let it be so; still it is at least quite certain that it seems to me that I see light, that I hear noise and that I feel heat. That cannot be false; properly speaking it is what is in me called *feeling*; and used in this precise sense that is no other thing than thinking."[53]

Nonhuman animals do not seem to possess the ability to reason as evidenced by the fact that they do not communicate with language as do humans.[54] Thus, if a thinking thing is that which reasons and feels, and nonhuman animals are not rational, then they must also lack consciousness, and they have no moral status.

Despite the popular idea that Descartes believed animals to be unconscious machines, some of his writings show that this was not necessarily the case.[55] In some places, Descartes shows that he thought it obvious that

---

51. Descartes, *Discourse on Method*, 4.
52. Harrison, "Descartes on Animals," 222.
53. Descartes, *Discourse on Method*, 66 (emphasis added).
54. Descartes, *Discourse on Method*, 5.
55. Harrison, "Descartes on Animals," 219–27; Cottingham, "Decartes' Treatment of

some nonhuman animals are conscious. For example, in a letter to Henry More, Descartes clarifies,

> For brevity's sake I here omit the other reasons for denying thought to animals. Please note that I am speaking of thought, and not of life or sensation. I do not deny life to animals, since I regard it as consisting simply in the heat of the heart; and I do not even deny sensation, in so far as it depends on a bodily organ.[56]

So, Descartes did not completely reject the possibility of nonhuman animal consciousness. It seems he believed that nonhuman animals had a consciousness explained completely in physical terms in contrast to human consciousness, which was explained in terms of both the material and immaterial.[57]

Contemporary Opponents

Neo-Cartesians

Whatever Descartes's genuine view on nonhuman animals and despite the philosophical and scientific problems facing Cartesian dualism, there have been many philosophers who have held viewpoints similar to Descartes.[58] In his work *The Problem of Pain*, C. S. Lewis says that animals do not experience pain in a morally significant way. Lewis believed that animals do not experience pain through successive moments of time because they lack self-consciousness. His oft-quoted statement explains this belief:

> There is, therefore, I take it, no question of immortality for creatures that are merely sentient. Nor do justice and mercy demand that there should be, for such creatures have no painful experience. Their nervous system delivers all the *letters* A, P, N, I, but since they cannot read they never build it up into the world PAIN. And all animals *may* be in that condition.[59]

Animals," 225–33.

56. See his "Letter to More, 5 February 1649" in Descartes, *Philosophical Writings of Descartes*, 366.

57. Harrison, "Descartes on Animals," 224.

58. For a detailed discussion of Neo-Cartesianism, see Murray, *Nature Red in Tooth and Claw*, 41–72.

59. Lewis, *Problem of Pain*, 142 (emphasis in original).

Nonhuman animals, without a subjective something that unites all of their successive pain sensations, do not own pain in the sense that humans do. They cannot think of themselves as the subjects of even a single instance of pain. So, although Lewis assumed that animals feel pain, he sought to answer the problem of animal suffering by emphasizing their lack of subjectivity.

Peter Harrison, in "Theodicy and Animal Pain," provides a stronger defense of the ideas found in Lewis's writings. Harrison seems to get closer to Descartes in that Harrison sheds doubt on the existence of pain consciousness in animals.[60] Harrison argues that if animal development is driven by evolution, then the subjective sensation of pain is not as important as behavior in regard to survival. He says the behavior of avoiding physical harm alone would be sufficient for flourishing, and perhaps animals do not feel or are not conscious of pain at all. This would be similar to the reactions of most people when they accidentally touch a hot stove; they immediately react by pulling their hand away without feeling pain.

Harrison also further develops the argument that pain in animals lacks moral significance without subjective continuity.[61] He provides examples illustrating why this is so. Among others, he says that people do not remember the pain they experienced as infants, and, therefore, they cannot be said to be the subject or owner of those experiences. He also says there would seem to be no morally significant difference between undergoing an operation with an anesthetic or with a hypothetical drug that would not block pain but would erase the memory of the patient after the procedure.

Christopher Southgate

Theologian Christopher Southgate, who originally trained in biochemistry, contributes to the discussion of the problem of animal suffering in his work *The Groaning of Creation: God, Evolution, and the Problem of Evil*.[62] In this book, Southgate considers the problem from a Neo-Darwinian evolutionary perspective. As the title indicates, Southgate's project is somewhat based on the apostle Paul's words in Romans 8:19–23 (NASB):

---

60. Harrison, "Theodicy and Animal Pain," 83–87.
61. Harrison, "Theodicy and Animal Pain," 87–92.
62. Southgate, *Groaning of Creation*.

> For the anxious longing of the creation waits eagerly for the revealing of the sons of God. For the creation was subjected to futility, not willingly, but because of Him who subjected it, in hope that the creation itself also will be set free from its slavery to corruption into the freedom of the glory of the children of God. For we know that the whole creation groans and suffers the pains of childbirth together until now. And not only this, but also we ourselves, having the first fruits of the Spirit, even we ourselves groan within ourselves, waiting eagerly for our adoption as sons, the redemption of our body.

Southgate takes creation's subjection "to futility" as a subjection to evolutionary processes. However, he takes into account that God said creation was "very good" in Genesis 1. Given this, Southgate's main goal is to formulate an evolutionary theodicy that attempts to explain how a loving Trinitarian God could use these evolutionary processes resulting in a creation that is both "very good" and "groaning." However, in places he suggests that his project is not necessarily a definitive solution to the problem of animal suffering but more of a satisfactory explanation or description of God's involvement in the problem.[63]

Southgate discusses a few strategies for formulating theodicies involving evolutionary processes. He calls these strategies *good-harm analyses* (GHA), which are differing ways of balancing perceived goods and harms while proposing a theodicy. The three good-harm analyses Southgate discusses are *Property-consequence GHAs*, *Developmental GHAs*, and *Constitutive GHAs*.[64] Southgate concludes that a developmental good-harm analysis is the preferred strategy, given evolution, because it balances goods and harms by claiming that "the good is a goal that can only develop through a process which includes the possibility (or necessity) of harm."[65] He calls this first step in his evolutionary theodicy the *only way argument* in which he assumes that perhaps evolutionary processes were the only way in which God could "give rise to the sort of beauty, diversity, sentience, and sophistication of creatures that the biosphere now contains."[66]

Southgate emphasizes his belief that God (including the Father and Holy Spirit, not just the Son) suffers along with every animal (including humans) God creates. To explain God's use of evolutionary processes,

63. See Southgate, *Groaning of Creation*, 15–16.
64. Southgate, *Groaning of Creation*, 41.
65. Southgate, *Groaning of Creation*, 41.
66. Southgate, *Groaning of Creation*, 16; cf. 48.

Southgate suggests that God relinquishes a degree of control over the universe similar to the self-emptying of Christ in his assumption of a human nature. All of this helps explain how God can be viewed as loving his creation and creatures alongside subjecting them to evolutionary processes. For example, Southgate explains,

> Theologically we may posit that the frustration of the creature, be it of the insurance pelican chick, or the sheep parasitized by the worm *Redia*, or the aging lion beaten for the first time in a fight with a younger male, is received by the Son through the brooding immanence of the Spirit, and uttered in that Spirit as a song of lament to the Father. All that the frustrated creature suffers, and all it might have been but for frustration, is retained in the memory of the Trinity.[67]

Thus, assuming that evolutionary processes were the "only way" to give rise to the good in creation, each Person of the Trinity is seen co-suffering with creatures as they experience the suffering involved with natural selection.

Southgate also discusses God's involvement in evolution and Christ's crucifixion to avoid promoting a deistic theology. He suggests that God somehow places parameters on the evolutionary process resulting in humanity. This prohibits the idea that rewinding the evolutionary clock and replaying evolutionary history could result in different numbers and kinds of species on Earth.

Michael Murray and Glenn Ross

In 2006, Michael Murray and Glenn Ross published their article titled "Neo-Cartesianism and the Problem of Animal Suffering."[68] The arguments in that article later served as a major aspect of Murray's defense of theism in his work on the problem of animal suffering titled *Nature Red in Tooth and Claw: Theism and the Problem of Animal Suffering*.[69] Murray's book was especially significant at the time because few, if any, monographs had been published covering the problem of animal suffering.[70]

---

67. Southgate, *Groaning of Creation*, 65.

68. Murray and Ross, "Neo-Cartesianism and the Problem of Animal Suffering," 169–90.

69. Murray, *Nature Red in Tooth and Claw*.

70. Christopher Southgate's work was published the same year.

The Problem of Animal Suffering

The argument in "Neo-Cartesianism and the Problem of Animal Suffering," inspired by René Descartes, emphasizes that there is no evidence proving that nonhuman animals phenomenologically experience pain. Murray and Ross argue that although some nonhuman animals have physiological systems analogous to the systems in humans that make the phenomenological experience of pain possible, there is no evidence necessitating the conclusion that nonhuman animals do phenomenologically experience pain.[71] They suggest it is possible that nonhuman animals exhibit pain-averse behaviors although nonhuman animals might not phenomenologically experience pain. Murray and Ross mention it does not seem that the actual awareness of pain would add to the evolutionary advantage of pain-avoiding behaviors.[72] Thus, if one has good reasons to believe that theism is true, then there is room to believe that nonhuman animals do not phenomenologically experience pain since it would seem that God would not allow them to do so.[73]

Murray and Ross discuss four similar, but different, options from which neo-Cartesians can choose regarding animals and pain:

1. Many nonhuman creatures are conscious inasmuch as they are alive, awake and have sensations.... Yet, unlike the sensory states possessed by humans, the mechanisms whereby these organisms have access to the world lack any phenomenal character whatsoever;[74]

2. For a mental state to be a conscious state (phenomenally) requires an accompanying higher-order mental state (a HOT) that has that state as its intentional object.... Only humans have the cognitive faculties required to form the conception of themselves being in a first-order state that one must have in order to have a HOT;[75]

3. Some nonhuman creatures have states that have intrinsic phenomenal qualities analogous to those possessed by humans when they are in

---

71. Murray and Ross emphasize that they do not necessarily believe neo-Cartesianism to be true but that the possibility of its truth is significant for the problem of animal suffering (Murray and Ross, "Neo-Cartesianism and the Problem of Animal Suffering," 186).

72. Murray and Ross, "Neo-Cartesianism and the Problem of Animal Suffering," 177.

73. Murray and Ross, "Neo-Cartesianism and the Problem of Animal Suffering," 171–72, 186.

74. Murray and Ross, "Neo-Cartesianism and the Problem of Animal Suffering," 175.

75. Murray and Ross, "Neo-Cartesianism and the Problem of Animal Suffering," 176.

states of pain. These creatures lack, however, any higher-order states of being aware of themselves as being in first-order states;[76] and

4. Most creatures lack the cognitive faculties required to be in a higher-order state of recognizing themselves to be in a first-order state of pain. Those nonhuman creatures that can on occasion achieve a second-order access to their first-order states of pain, nonetheless do not have the capacity to regard that second-order state as undesirable.[77]

So, according to Murray and Ross, neo-Cartesianism entails that animals either (1) lack phenomenal consciousness, (2) lack the higher-order mental states required for phenomenal consciousness, (3) are phenomenally conscious of pain but lack higher-order mental states, or (4) are phenomenally aware of pain and some have higher-order mental states regarding the pain but lack the capacity to regard such higher states as undesirable. If any one of these four options were true, then the apparent suffering found in nature would be illusory, and the problem of animal suffering would dissolve.

In *Nature Red in Tooth and Claw*, after explaining and evaluating neo-Cartesianism, Murray goes on to discuss additional solutions to the problem of animal suffering.[78] These involve concepts such as the nature of nonhuman animal pain and flourishing, the nature of natural evil, and the possible necessity of fixed physical laws. Here he explains *nomic-regularity arguments* that claim God must create an ordered universe in order to actualize God's purposes. Murray adds to the nomic-regularity arguments by proposing and defending the idea that God must not only create a universe regularly governed by laws, but also this universe must form from chaos to order. He discusses historical theistic arguments for the intrinsic goodness of a universe that forms from chaos to order:

> From Augustine to Van Till there is a substantial thread of thought in the Christian-theistic tradition arguing for the importance not only of nomic regularity but also of CTO [chaos to order]. Were this line of thought to emerge only after 1859, one might find the defense of CTO merely ad hoc. It did not. The fundamental claim defended by all of these figures is simply that a universe which acts as a machine-making machine, producing substantial amounts of

---

76. Murray and Ross, "Neo-Cartesianism and the Problem of Animal Suffering," 176.
77. Murray and Ross, "Neo-Cartesianism and the Problem of Animal Suffering," 177.
78. Murray, *Nature Red in Tooth and Claw*, 107–92.

aesthetic, moral, and religious value over time, is of greater value than creation of the finished project by divine fiat.[79]

Murray ultimately suggests that combining these solutions makes for a compelling case against the problem of animal suffering. He argues,

> For all we know, however, animal pain and suffering might be explained in part by each of the following:
>
> (1) The good of a world in which there are nonhuman animals capable of good, spontaneous, and intentional actions.
>
> (2) The good of preserving organismic integrity in a world where animals are liable to physical harm.
>
> (3) The good of an eternal existence where animals can enjoy, in limited respects, the goodness of the presence of God.
>
> (4) The good of a nominally regular world which supports free and effective choice, intellectual inquiry, and a good and diverse created order.
>
> (5) The good of a universe which moves from chaos to order.[80]

Murray never attempts to provide a theodicy that fully explains the compatibility of God and animal suffering but simply attempts to provide a minimal defense that shows, "for all we know," God might have a good reason for allowing nonhuman animal suffering. He concludes that this is sufficient to deflect the problem and sustain the rationality and coherence of theism.

Nicola Hoggard Creegan

Theologian Nicola Creegan took a similar route as Southgate with her 2013 work titled *Animal Suffering and the Problem of Evil*.[81] In this book, Creegan attempts to formulate a theodicy answering the problem of evil, regarding nonhuman animal suffering in particular, in light of evolutionary processes. Her main argument considers concepts from evolutionary theory and involves viewing creation in light of Jesus' parable of the wheat and tares.

The basis of her argument is that the traditional understanding that evil exists in the world due to human sin is outdated in light of evolutionary

---

79. Murray, *Nature Red in Tooth and Claw*, 183.
80. Murray, *Nature Red in Tooth and Claw*, 196–97.
81. Creegan, *Animal Suffering and the Problem of Evil*.

theory.[82] However, she says that Jesus' parable of the wheat and tares is the key to understanding how Christians might be able to formulate a theodicy in light of this.[83] Creegan argues this parable can be expanded to include all of nature. Understood in this way, evolutionary processes involving suffering and death are viewed as the work of some evil influence and not God. She says that although we see evil, death, and suffering in evolutionary history and today, we can still know that God is good when viewing the perfections in nature alongside the imperfections.

Creegan uses concepts from evolutionary theory, such as symbiosis, evo devo, and emergence, to argue that evolution does not necessarily entail the traditional understanding that it is solely an unguided process.[84] So, although evolutionary processes involve evil, Christians should not blame this on God but instead should realize that God is working behind the scenes, along with an evil influence mentioned by Jesus in the parable. Evil and suffering are real, and are involved in the very formulation of mankind, but are not directly caused by God and will one day be eliminated.

Trent Dougherty

The last monograph dedicated to the problem of animal suffering under discussion is Trent Dougherty's *The Problem of Animal Pain: A Theodicy for All Creatures Great and Small*.[85] Dougherty takes a different approach to the problem from his contemporaries and attempts to answer the problem through a soul-making theodicy. He believes that theists have too easily dismissed such an approach in the past.

Dougherty's argument basically states that if God is all-good and all-loving, then God would see to it that nonhuman animals participate in an afterlife in which they are granted rationality and self-awareness and are able to reflect on their earthly lives. He states his thesis clearly in his introduction:

> I will defend the thesis that a class of animals (to be discussed later) will not only be resurrected at the eschaton, but will be deified in much the same way that humans will be. That they will become, in the language of Narnia, "talking animals." . . . So I am suggesting that they will become full-fledged persons (rational

---

82. Creegan, *Animal Suffering and the Problem of Evil*, 14–43.
83. Creegan, *Animal Suffering and the Problem of Evil*, 91–96.
84. Creegan, *Animal Suffering and the Problem of Evil*, 110–26.
85. Dougherty, *Problem of Animal Pain*.

substances) who can look back on their lives—both pre- and post-personal—and form attitudes about what has happened to them and how they fit into God's plan. If God is just and loving, and if they are rational and of good will, then they will accept, though with no loss of the sense of gravity of their suffering, that they were an important part of something infinitely valuable, and that in addition to being justly, lavishly rewarded for it, they will embrace their role in creation. In this embrace, evil is defeated.[86]

Dougherty believes that the nonhuman animal participation in an afterlife makes it so that the good will greatly outweigh the bad in the lives of nonhuman animals. Dougherty formulates what he calls the *Transcendental Argument for Animal Deification*:

1. Animals have sentience.
2. Animals are made in the image of God.
3. Animals have moral standing.
4. God is all-powerful and perfectly loving, overflowing with love and concern for everything with moral standing.
5. God will do justly and lovingly by animals. That is, he will not allow harm to come to them that is not somehow compensated for, he will see to it that their existences are on the whole quite good (more than just better than on balance good) and that any suffering can be defeated within the context of their lives.
6. The only way God could do justly and lovingly by animals is to enfold their suffering in a greater good that organically defeats their evil.
7. The only way God could enfold animal suffering into some greater good that organically defeated it is either (i) via their relation to cosmic order, (ii) this-worldly soul-making, or (iii) other-worldly soul-making.
8. The argument from cosmic order is almost completely unsuccessful as it stands.
9. This-worldly soul-making cannot occur to a significant degree due to current lack of TTPU [transtemporal psychic unity] and other cognitive capacities.

---

86. Dougherty, *Problem of Animal Pain*, 3.

10. The only way God could enfold animal suffering into some greater good is via future soul-making.
11. The only way God could do justly and lovingly by animals is via future soul-making.
12. Future soul-making requires both animal resurrection and deification.
13. The only way God could do justly and lovingly by animals involves both animal resurrection and deification.
14. If God exists, then animals will be resurrected and deified.[87]

Dougherty's soul-making theodicy entails that God's allowance of human and nonhuman animal suffering makes it possible for certain moral traits (e.g., courage, fortitude, generosity, kindness) to be developed by those who face moral and natural evil. However, some sentient beings, especially nonhuman animals, experience so much suffering that their lives, on the whole, are dominated by evil. Thus, God must make it so that all sentient beings experience an afterlife as persons so they will be able to reflect on and embrace their earthly role in God's plan. Since all animals (human and nonhuman) will experience an afterlife, the possibility of cultivating soul-making traits will be available to all.

The Current Status of the Problem

There is no consensus on the problem of animal suffering right now, and the situation for theists seems to be one of disarray. Most, if not all, nontheists are unconvinced by arguments that have been proposed to answer the problem of animal suffering. Of course, to state that a nontheist is unconvinced by a theistic argument is almost a truism. However, even the opponents of the problem of animal suffering do not find each other's arguments convincing.

In 2013, philosopher Robert Francescotti surveyed the problem and concluded, mainly considering Murray's arguments, that the problem remains a serious concern for theists. Francescotti concludes,

> the Neo-Cartesian defenses fail to meet the standard of *not being significantly likely to be false,* and at least for the majority of knowledgeable individuals, they also fail to meet Murray's lax standard of *not conflicting with one's justified acceptances.* . . . So it

---

87. Dougherty, *Problem of Animal Pain,* 145.

The Problem of Animal Suffering

> seems that rather than denying the presence of animal suffering, a convincing defense will need to acknowledge its existence and explain why God would allow it. Yet, as argued in the previous section, the explanation that appeals to NR [nomic regularity] along with the progression of the universe from CTO [chaos to order] requires all of the animal suffering that actually does and did obtain, and it also seems quite likely that a lot of this suffering is not required.... So I will not conclude with confidence that animal suffering proves God's existence unlikely, but only that those who wish to convince themselves and others that it does not do so certainly need a stronger defense than what has been provided.[88]

Francescotti not only thinks that Murray's neo-Cartesian and nomic-regularity/chaos-to-order arguments fail to meet Murray's minimum standard, but also that combining animal suffering theodicies makes them more likely to be false. Francescotti argues,

> we must keep in mind that adding potential goods to the set of reasons for animal suffering threatens to render the entire conjunction less likely to be true than it already is. For instance, "God allows animal suffering for the sake of NR and CTO *and* increased delight in an animal afterlife" is less likely to be true than "God allows animal suffering for the sake of NR and CTO." The worry, then, is that while adding more reasons to the combined set makes it more likely that the Necessity Condition is met, the combined set of explanations is less likely to be true than any subset.[89]

As mentioned, Murray argues that combining theodicies makes for a more convincing case against the problem of animal suffering. However, Francescotti believes that combining theodicies actually makes their probability much less than their stand-alone probabilities.

Regardless of the opinion of nontheists, the most prominent opponents of the problem of animal suffering do not agree with one another and find each other's arguments highly unconvincing. For example, both Creegan and Dougherty devote space in their books to objecting to Murray's neo-Cartesian and nomic-regularity arguments.[90] For example, Creegan writes,

---

88. Francescotti, "Problem of Animal Pain and Suffering," 125–26 (emphasis in original).

89. Francescotti, "Problem of Animal Pain and Suffering," 126.

90. Creegan, *Animal Suffering and the Problem of Evil*, 51–53; Dougherty, *Problem of Animal Pain*, 77–95.

Murray's "chaos to order" universe, although convincing at one level, is less so at another because if God is to be the object of worship then God must be evident in the here and now, in the suffering and the pain and the numinous, and not just in the overall picture though such a picture is in the life of faith.[91]

In keeping with her theodicy, Creegan believes that Murray too quickly rejects arguments regarding Satan as a major cause of evil. She argues that Murray's defense needs to consider a more direct cause of evil that God continually struggles to defeat (and will eventually defeat).

Dougherty spends a chapter arguing against Murray's neo-Cartesian arguments.[92] Drawing evidence and arguments from science, the philosophy of language, and the philosophy of mind and animal minds, Dougherty argues that there are more options for understanding how nonhuman animals experience pain than Murray discussed in *Nature Red in Tooth and Claw*. Since most concerned scientists believe that nonhuman animal suffering is morally significant, it is reasonable to believe that it is. Moreover, higher-order thought theories of consciousness over-intellectualize the process of determining whether nonhuman animals are aware of their pain in some way. Pain is more of an emotion than a concept, and it is likely that nonhuman animals are aware of their pain, even if they are not aware of themselves as persons.

Elsewhere, Murray argues that there are problems with Dougherty's theodicy.[93] He argues that Dougherty offers an animal soul-making theodicy that seems to contradict the very *raison d'être* of soul-making theodicies. For example, although Dougherty provides plenty of argumentation as to why God should resurrect animals in the eschaton, he does not explain how the earthly lives of animals can give rise to personality traits that cannot surface without the existence of actual or possible suffering.[94]

Although Creegan's and Southgate's works are not debated among Creegan, Dougherty, Murray, and Southgate, their works do not provide complete explanations for evil. For example, Southgate mentions that his arguments are not necessarily meant to solve the problem of animal suffering but merely explain why God cannot prevent or eliminate nonhuman

---

91. Creegan, *Animal Suffering and the Problem of Evil*, 53.
92. Dougherty, *Problem of Animal Pain*, 77–95.
93. Murray, Review of *Problem of Animal Pain*, 137–41.
94. Murray, Review of *Problem of Animal Pain*, 138.

animal suffering.[95] Similarly, Creegan does not offer a theodicy because she thinks we may never fully understand why evil exists in creation.[96] Even if their explanations were complete, Creegan and Southgate do not technically provide theodicies because their arguments involve a God who is not all-powerful as God has been classically understood. In other words, their answers to the problem of animal suffering concede that the God of classical theism does not, in fact, exist.

In short, there have been four recent, major treatments from theists covering the problem of animal suffering (i.e., Murray, Southgate, Creegan, Dougherty). Out of the four, two of them include mere discussions of the problem without conclusive defenses. The remaining two include opposing answers that each of their adjacent authors reject. Of course, it is not necessary for there to be a consensus among theists for the problem of animal suffering to be defended, and disagreements are to be expected in any debate. However, it is striking that there are few, if any, nontheists who find theistic defenses of the problem of animal suffering convincing and that the opponents of the problem believe each other's arguments to be so ineffective. Indeed, some theists have even argued that the problem is probably worse than many have thought.[97]

The Problem of Animal Suffering: A Thomistic Theodicy

With this situation in mind, in this book, I will attempt to answer the problem of animal suffering from a different perspective of the four major, contemporary opponents of the problem of animal suffering. In particular, I will explain and expand upon the thought of the medieval philosopher/theologian Thomas Aquinas. In chapter 2, I will attempt to provide reasons for believing that both premises of Rowe's evidential argument are false. Regarding premise (1), I will first touch on something that has been missing from the debate over animal suffering: the very nature of nonhuman animal pain itself. Here I will explain Aquinas's privation view of evil and what it entails for Aquinas's views of pain and suffering in nonhuman animals. In particular, I will show that Aquinas's view of evil entails that animal suffering is not evil. Regarding premise (2), I will explain Aquinas's views of God's goodness and the human limitation on knowledge of God in

---

95. Southgate, *Groaning of Creation*, 15–17.
96. Creegan, *Animal Suffering and the Problem of Evil*, 55.
97. Crummett, "Problem of Evil and the Suffering of Creeping Things," 71–88.

this life. Here I will discuss how Aquinas's view of God entails that we can never know how God *should* act in any given situation.

Chapter 2 will raise the question of how animal suffering can be metaphysically good despite the nonhuman animal experience of pain and suffering. So, in chapter 3, I will expound on Aquinas's understanding of nonhuman animal minds. It is sometimes believed that Aquinas thinks nonhuman animal suffering is morally insignificant merely because nonhuman animals are arational. This is not true. In this chapter, I will explain how Aquinas's concept of the rational soul includes not only rationality, but also self-awareness; nonhuman animal suffering is not morally significant not only because nonhuman animals are arational, but also because they lack self-awareness. These two chapters, I believe, provide the keys to answering Rowe's argument.

Next, in chapter 4, I will turn to Draper's inference-to-the-best-explanation arguments from animal suffering. As Draper argues that naturalism better explains the world we experience, I will discuss Aquinas's arguments regarding why God created a hierarchy of contingent beings. In this discussion, I will expound on Aquinas's arguments regarding God's reason for creating and the implications this purpose has for the universe God wills to create. This discussion will show that the classical theism of Aquinas does a much better job than naturalism at explaining the world we observe.

In chapter 5, I will attempt to provide an answer to the idea that God is morally obligated to initially create a paradise for nonhuman animals and humanity. This idea is prevalent in the literature of young-earth creationists and also seems to be the driving force of many arguments against God from animal suffering. Indeed, if a long process of animal death and suffering is supposed to be evidence against God's existence, this seems to entail that God is obligated to directly create a world without suffering. In this chapter, I will explain how several Thomistic concepts from previous chapters can be used to show that God is not morally obligated to create a world that initially is free of evil.

After this, I have included an appendix covering a topic that does not necessarily concern the problem of animal suffering yet is pertinent to defending Aquinas's theodicy. The appendix will discuss Stephen Law's evil-god challenge. The *evil-god challenge* is an argument stating that all theodicies, including Aquinas's, fail because they are no more probable than anti-theodicies. I will discuss Law's challenge, along with John Collins's extension of it, and show how Aquinas's metaphysics answer the challenge.

The Problem of Animal Suffering

All of these Thomistic arguments against the problem of animal suffering will show that the problem of animal suffering fails, and nonhuman animal suffering is morally insignificant; nonhuman animal suffering does not count as evidence against God's existence. Also, Aquinas's philosophical theology shows that God created the world for a very different purpose from the one most atheists assume. Given this purpose, theism is coherent regarding its understanding of God's attributes and the existence of nonhuman animal suffering.

2

The Nature of Animal Suffering and God's Goodness[1]

THE PROBLEM OF ANIMAL suffering is usually categorized as a type of *evidential problem of evil*. The evidential problem of evil emphasizes, as mentioned, that there exist instances of gratuitous evil that God should not allow to occur. Once again, William Rowe's argument states,

1. There exist instances of intense suffering which an omnipotent, omniscient being could have prevented without thereby losing some greater good or permitting some evil equally bad or worse.

2. An omniscient, wholly good being would prevent the occurrence of any intense suffering it could, unless it could not do so without thereby losing some greater good or permitting some evil equally bad or worse.

3. There does not exist an omnipotent, omniscient, wholly good being.[2]

Rowe emphasizes that, while it is uncertain whether any cases of animal suffering are pointless, it is rational to assume that at least some are pointless given the great amount that occur in the world.[3] This is said to be an evidential problem because the great number of instances of suffering

1. Major portions of this chapter were taken from Keltz, "Is Animal Suffering Evil?," 1–19.

2. Rowe, "Problem of Evil and Some Varieties of Atheism," 336.

3. "The truth is that we are not in a position to prove that (1) is true. We cannot know with certainty that instances of suffering of the sort described in (1) do occur in our world. But it is one thing to know or prove that (1) is true and quite another thing to have rational grounds for believing (1) to be true" (Rowe, "Problem of Evil and Some Varieties of Atheism," 337).

increases the probability of the problem being true. The vast amount of intense, nonhuman animal suffering in the past and present provides overwhelming evidence to conclude that some of these instances of suffering are pointless (although it is difficult, if not impossible, to know if there is a good reason for God to allow each case of intense suffering in the world).

Many articles and monographs have been written in the attempt to answer Rowe's evidential problem.[4] One example, Stephen Wykstra's response to Rowe in 1984, gave rise to a new position in the philosophy of religion known as *skeptical theism*.[5] Skeptical theism is the position that for any given case of apparent pointless suffering, for all we know, there is a good reason for God to allow such suffering. It is never certain that any particular case of intense suffering is pointless because no one is in a position to know the depths of God's knowledge about the world and the goods he produces. Just because the fawn's suffering seems pointless, it does not follow that there is a good that does not come from it or that it did not prevent something equally bad or worse.

Most of the discussion has involved premise (1) and the question of whether nonhuman animal suffering is gratuitous. It is assumed that nonhuman animal suffering is evil regardless of whether it is pointless, and it is assumed that God would not allow gratuitous nonhuman animal suffering. However, if it could be shown that nonhuman animal suffering is not evil, then both premise (1) and premise (2) will be proven false.

In the first half of this chapter, I will explore the natures of pain and suffering from a Thomistic perspective to argue that nonhuman animal suffering is not evil. First, I will discuss Aquinas's evil-as-privation view and his understanding of pain and suffering. I will show that although they are the products of medieval philosophy, Aquinas's concepts of pain and suffering are not contradictory to their contemporary philosophical and scientific counterparts. Afterward, I will explain that pain and suffering are not evil; they are metaphysically good in that they exist and are exactly what God intends them to be in nonhuman animals.

While Aquinas's evil-as-privation view answers both premises of Rowe's argument, I will also argue that premise (2) is false for metaphysical and epistemological reasons. In the second half of this chapter, I will

---

4. Graham Oppy provides a good discussion of Rowe's evidential argument and a list for further reading. See Oppy, "Rowe's Evidential Arguments from Evil," 49–66.

5. Wykstra, "Humean Obstacle to Evidential Arguments from Suffering," 73–93. See McBrayer, "Skeptical Theism," 611–23; and Dougherty and McBrayer, *Skeptical Theism: New Essays*.

discuss Aquinas's understanding of God's goodness, infinity, and transcendence and why Aquinas thinks we cannot know whether God is obligated to prevent nonhuman animal suffering—even gratuitous suffering. Finally, I will discuss the implications that this conclusion has for the problem of animal suffering. I will conclude that, regardless of whether nonhuman animal suffering is gratuitous, it is impossible to know whether God should prevent suffering.

Considering the Nature of Animal Suffering

Although intense discussion of the problem of animal suffering is relatively recent, it is striking that the nature of pain and suffering are rarely examined. Instead, it is often assumed that pain and suffering are evils that a loving God would not allow without good reason. An illustration of this is William Rowe's argument in "The Problem of Evil and Some Varieties of Atheism." Again, he states,

> In developing the argument for atheism based on the existence of evil, it will be useful to focus on some particular evil that our world contains in considerable abundance. Intense human and animal suffering, for example, occurs daily and in great plenitude in our world. Such intense suffering is a clear case of evil.[6]

Here it is notable that, without argument, Rowe claims human and nonhuman animal suffering in the world is a "clear case of evil." As mentioned earlier, this leads to his famous fawn-in-the-woods example in which a fawn is caught in a forest fire, trapped by a tree, horribly burned, and finally dies in agony after several days. Rowe argues that the fawn's suffering would be pointless:

> So far as we can see, the fawn's intense suffering is pointless. For there does not appear to be any greater good such that the prevention of the fawn's suffering would require either the loss of that good or the occurrence of an evil equally bad or worse. Nor does there seem to be an equally bad or worse evil so connected to the fawn's suffering that it would have had to occur had the fawn's suffering been prevented.[7]

---

6. Rowe, "Problem of Evil and Some Varieties of Atheism," 335.
7. Rowe, "Problem of Evil and Some Varieties of Atheism," 337.

Notably, Rowe again is assuming that the pain and suffering in this example are self-evidently evil.

Yet it is not just the proponents of the problem of animal suffering who assume nonhuman animal pain and suffering are evil. In *Nature Red in Tooth and Claw*, Michael Murray also discusses nonhuman animal suffering as an evil that God cannot allow without a good reason. For example, in a chapter titled, "Neo-Cartesianism," he discusses philosophers who have argued that nonhuman animals do not phenomenologically experience pain and suffering.[8] Murray discusses these arguments because, as he emphasizes, "if there is no such thing as animal pain and suffering, there is no such thing as an argument *from it* to atheism."[9] Thus, although Murray provides an almost exhaustive treatment of the problem, he never discusses why it would be evil for God to allow nonhuman animals to undergo pain and suffering.

It seems that as the debate stands, all parties assume that nonhuman animal pain and suffering are evils that an all-good God should not allow without a good reason. For example, while surveying the problem, Robert Francescotti mentions,

> denying the existence of a certain sort of evil rather than explaining why God allows its existence is an effective strategy only when it is clear that the evil does not exist, and there is very good reason to believe that many other animals experience phenomenally distressful states. So it seems that rather than denying the presence of animal suffering, a convincing defense will need to acknowledge its existence and explain why God would allow it.[10]

Yet this quote is striking because it is evidence that there is a debate within the philosophy of religion that is partly based on an assumption. This situation raises the question of whether pain and suffering are evil. This question is important because if pain and suffering are evil, then theists need to consider why God would allow them. However, if they are not evil, or if there is reason to doubt they are evil, then their existence will not necessarily add to the evidence against God.

---

8. Murray, *Nature Red in Tooth and Claw*, 41–72.
9. Murray, *Nature Red in Tooth and Claw*, 42 (emphasis in original).
10. Francescotti, "Problem of Animal Pain and Suffering," 125.

Thomism and the Problem of Animal Suffering

The Thomistic Concept of Evil

Aquinas discusses evil in many places in his writings, but probably defines it most clearly in his discussion in the *Summa theologiae* (*ST*): "evil is the absence of the good, which is natural and due to a thing."[11] This is a statement of Aquinas's famous evil-as-privation theory in which he believes that an evil is the absence of a good that should obtain. It is important to note that, according to Aquinas, not all absences of good are evil, although all evils are absences of some good. In this regard, he is careful to make a distinction between *negative* and *privative* absences of good.[12] Aquinas explains,

> Absence of good, taken negatively, is not evil; otherwise, it would follow that what does not exist is evil, and also that everything would be evil, through not having the good belonging to something else; for instance, a man would be evil who had not the swiftness of the roe, or the strength of a lion. But the absence of good, taken in a privative sense, is an evil; as, for instance, the privation of sight is called blindness.[13]

As can be seen in Aquinas's definition of *evil*, an absence of a good is only evil if the absence of good is "natural and due" to a particular subject. For example, it would be an evil for a human to be blind because sight is something humans should possess according to their natures. But it would not be an evil for a rock to lack vision as rocks do not naturally possess the ability to see.[14] The absence of sight in a human is a privation of a natural good, and the absence of sight in a rock is merely a negative absence of a good.

Aquinas mentions two main types of evils that correspond to what are referred to today as "natural evils" and "moral evils."[15] For example, he says,

> In one way it [evil] occurs by the subtraction of the form, or of any part required for the integrity of the thing, as blindness is an evil, as also it is an evil to be wanting in any member of the body. In another way evil exists by the withdrawal of the due operation, either because it does not exist, or because it has not its due mode and order. But because good in itself is the object of the will, evil,

---

11. *ST* I, q. 49, a. 1.
12. *ST* I, q. 48, a. 3; see also *De Malo*, q. 1, a. 2.
13. *ST* I, q. 48, a. 3.
14. *ST* I, q. 48, a. 5, ad1.
15. *ST* I, q. 48, a. 5; *De Malo*, q. 1, a. 4.

which is the privation of good, is found in a special way in rational creatures which have a will.[16]

Natural evils include things such as disease and death, which entail "subtractions" of the forms of the organisms they affect. Moral evils are actions that rational creatures choose to do, which are "withdrawals" from the way they ought to act in accord with their natures.

It may be unclear as to how Aquinas would classify pain and suffering. Most would probably assume that he would classify pain and suffering as evils. But a close examination of Aquinas's writings shows that this is not necessarily the case.

The Thomistic Concepts of Pain and Suffering

Pain and suffering seem to provide an interesting problem for Thomism because of Aquinas's doctrine that evil is a privation of the good. Pain and suffering are very real and unpleasant experiences that do not qualify as privations in the same way in which do blindness, paralysis, and death. The experiences of pain and suffering are actualized through the physiological processes in humans and animals.

Indeed, philosophers have argued that the existence of pain and suffering shows that the privation theory of evil is incorrect. G. Stanley Kane argues that the nature of pain proves the privation theory wrong because pain is an evil, yet not a privation.[17] In addition, Mark Robson argues that some types of suffering, such as depression and dread, provide evidence against the privation theory of evil.[18]

However, Aquinas would disagree with both philosophers. Although they do not directly interact with him, both Kane and Robson argue against the privation theory of evil without taking Aquinas's views on pain and suffering into account. The existence of pain and suffering would not in the least surprise Aquinas because, far from forgetting these things, he discusses them extensively in his writings. His discussions regarding pain and suffering clearly show that he did not view them as privations.

---

16. *ST* I, q. 48, a. 5; see *De Malo*, q. 1, a. 4.
17. Kane, "Evil and Privation," 49–51.
18. Robson, "Evil, Privation, Depression and Dread," 558–61.

In the *ST*, Aquinas commits five questions to the topic of pain and sorrow (*dolor* and *tristitia*).[19] He argues that pain is a type of emotion (*passio animae*).[20] For Aquinas, emotions are passive psychological states that affect the organism in which they subsist.[21] They are passive in that they do not usually arise without some type of cognition. Yet although they are passive, once aroused they can move an organism toward the object of cognition or away from it.

Aquinas refers to pain as a concupiscible emotion in the *ST*.[22] Concupiscible emotions are emotions that either move an organism toward something that is cognized as good, or away from something cognized as evil.[23] Pain moves an organism away from something cognized as evil. If the body perceives something on or in the body as evil, then the organism is averted from that evil.[24]

From this it is clear that Aquinas does not view pain as a privation. He believes that pain is a passive psychological state that affects an organism. This is not the absence of a good. He even argues that there are good aspects of pain. For example, he says,

> supposing the presence of something saddening or painful, it is a sign of goodness if a man is in sorrow or pain on account of this present evil. For if he were not to be in sorrow or pain, this could only be either because he feels it not, or because he does not reckon it as something unbecoming, both of which are manifest evils. Consequently it is a condition of goodness, that, supposing an evil to be present, sorrow or pain should ensue.[25]

So, Aquinas would definitely not think of pain as a privation. It cannot be an evil because it is a psychological state that is actualized in an organism through cognition. Moreover, without pain to move an organism away from a cognized evil, the evil would remain. Thus, to Aquinas, pain is not the absence of something that ought to be present in organisms, and it also seems to serve a purpose.

19. *ST* I-II, q. 35–39.
20. *ST* I-II, q. 35, a. 1.
21. For a brief overview of Aquinas's understanding of the emotions and how they compare to contemporary views on emotions see King, "Emotions," 209–26.
22. *ST* I-II, q. 23, a. 2.
23. *ST* I, q. 81, a. 2.
24. *ST* I-II, q. 36, a. 1.
25. *ST* I-II, q. 39, a. 1.

The Nature of Animal Suffering and God's Goodness

Aquinas discusses several types of emotions often associated with suffering. The three pertinent emotions he discusses are sorrow, despair, and fear (*tristitia*, *desperatio*, and *timor*).[26] Aquinas includes sorrow among the concupiscible emotions in the *ST*.[27] Specifically, he believes that sorrow is a different form of pain. He explains that both pain and sorrow are concupiscible emotions that avert an organism from things cognized as evil. However, he says the difference is that pain is cognized through the exterior senses (i.e., hearing, smell, taste, touch, and vision), while sorrow is cognized through the interior senses of the estimative power and the phantasia.[28]

Sorrow is an extension of pain because things cognized through the exterior senses can also be cognized through the interior senses. Pain itself can cause sorrow; yet sorrow is more far-reaching than pain because the thing cognized need not be conjoined with the organism as with the exterior senses. Sorrow arises in an organism when its interior senses cognize something as an evil that could deprive the organism of a good. The sorrow in turn averts the organism from the cognized evil.

Aquinas lists despair and fear among the irascible emotions in the *ST*.[29] Irascible emotions are distinguished from concupiscible emotions through the manner in which something is cognized.[30] Concupiscible emotions either attract or avert an organism when something is cognized as good or evil in itself. Irascible emotions arise in an organism when something is cognized as difficult in relation to the organism.

For example, hope results when something is cognized as a difficult good, yet attainable, because it is attracted somehow to the organism.[31] In contrast, despair results when something is cognized as a difficult good, yet unattainable, because it is averted somehow from the organism. In both cases, the organism is already attracted to the good, but the emotion arises through the perception that the good is difficult to obtain and is either attainable or not.

Fear is contrasted with despair in that something is cognized as a difficult evil. For example, fear results when something is cognized as a difficult

---

26. *ST* I-II, q. 35–39; q. 40, a. 4.
27. *ST* I-II, q. 36, a. 1.
28. *ST* I-II, q. 35, a. 2.
29. *ST* I-II, q. 23, a. 2.
30. *ST* I-II, q. 23, a. 1; *De Veritate*, q. 25, a. 2.
31. I borrow this and the following examples (hope, despair, fear, and confidence) used to explain the irascible emotions from King, "Emotions," 15.

evil that is unavoidable because it is attracted somehow to the organism. In contrast, confidence results when something is cognized as a difficult evil, yet avoidable, because it is averted somehow from the organism.

Similar to pain, Aquinas believes that there are good aspects of sorrow, despair, and fear. As sorrow is an extension of pain, it too is useful for moving organisms away from cognized evils.[32] Aquinas is not as specific in regard to goods that can come from the irascible emotions of despair and fear. However, he does hint at goods that can come from them.

For example, Aquinas mentions that despair can give rise to hope. He says, "Despair threatens danger in war, on account of a certain hope that attaches to it. For they who despair of flight, strive less to fly, but hope to avenge their death: and therefore in this hope they fight the more bravely, and consequently prove dangerous to the foe."[33] Here he is replying to the objection that despair is good in that it can invoke humans to become more dangerous when threatened. His reply is careful to emphasize that despair is not good in that it directly causes action, but in that it can give rise to hopes that themselves can cause action.

Elsewhere, Aquinas mentions that one of the good aspects of fear is that it can cause good actions. He mentions, "on the part of the soul, if the fear be moderate, without much disturbance of the reason, it conduces to working well, insofar as it causes a certain solicitude, and makes a man take counsel and work with greater attention."[34] So fear can add to the good of sorrow or distress in that it can add to the urgency of the aversion to a cognized evil.

Thus, Aquinas views neither pain nor other emotions attributed to suffering as privations of natural goods. They are all psychological states that have good aspects conducive to the good of the organism in which they arise. Even though Kane and Robson are not directly interacting with Aquinas, they both fail to realize that unpleasant emotions can be good.

Contemporary Views of Pain and Suffering

Although Aquinas was writing in the thirteenth century, his concepts of pain and suffering are not obsolete. Of course, there are several different philosophical and scientific theories regarding pain and suffering. However,

32. *ST* I-II, q. 39, a. 1.
33. *ST* I-II, q. 40, a. 8, ad3.
34. *ST* I-II, q. 44, a. 4.

The Nature of Animal Suffering and God's Goodness

among these there are a handful that cohere with Aquinas's understanding of pain and unpleasant emotions.

Today much has been learned about pain through the sciences and philosophy. It is understood that pain is a complex phenomenon that includes three different aspects: nociception, the sensation of pain, and the unpleasantness of pain.[35] Not all three are required for the experience of pain, but oftentimes most are present when pain is experienced.

Nociception is nerve activity activated by stimulus that is potentially damaging to an organism. It is purely a physiological process, distinguished from the sensation and unpleasantness of pain, because nociception is the name of the nerve activity before it is processed by higher centers of the nervous system.[36] Among other things, nociception is what makes it possible to reflexively move a hand or foot away from hot surfaces before any pain is experienced.

The sensation of pain is the next aspect of pain. This is the subjective experience of an imperative command from the body to protect a certain part of the body.[37] The sensation of pain is thought to be a homeostatic emotion, similar to itching, hunger, and thirst.[38] Pain sensations come in differing qualities and intensities. The quality of a pain sensation can either be aching, burning, stabbing, throbbing, etc. The intensity of the sensation of pain can be anything from mild to severe. The more intense the sensation is the more motivational force it will have on its subject.

The third aspect of pain is the unpleasantness of pain. Some might find it odd to distinguish between the sensation and the unpleasantness of pain because many people, including philosophers, think of all pains as unpleasant.[39] However, the distinction is necessary because reflection on the issue will reveal that there are pains that do not hurt, and there are also hurtful sensations that are not pains. For example, mild pains, similar to gently moving the tip of a needle across the skin, are not considered unpleasant.[40] Mild pains seem to be neither pleasant nor unpleasant and

---

35. Roughly similar to the four aspects described in Loeser, "Perspectives on Pain," 313; and Marchand, *Phenomenon of Pain*, 12.

36. Marchand, *Phenomenon of Pain*, 12.

37. Klein, *What the Body Commands*, 57.

38. Craig, "New View of Pain as a Homeostatic Emotion," 303–7.

39. For a survey of views entailing that all pains are unpleasant, see Swenson, "Intrinsic Value, Pain, and Method," 14–49.

40. Hare and Gardiner, "Pain and Evil," 97.

are merely neutral sensations. Also, sensations, such as thirst or hunger, can be considered unpleasant, although they are not pains.[41]

While the sensation of pain is understood (according to some theories) as an imperative command from the body regarding the protection of a part of the body, some philosophers believe that the unpleasantness of pain is a separate, imperative command from the body regarding the sensation of pain itself.[42] An example would be someone stepping on a tack with a bare foot. The imperative command from the sensation of pain would be something like, "Protect your foot!" The imperative command from the unpleasantness of the sensation would be similar to, "Don't have this sensation in your foot!"[43] It is believed that, while the sensation of pain motivates an organism to protect its body, the unpleasantness of pain motivates an organism to take action to end the sensation to regain the ability to perform actions naturally.[44]

Similar to pain, there is a long history of the study of emotions, and there are many competing theories of what exactly emotions are. One particular theory of emotions is that they are states evoked by rewarding stimuli and punishing stimuli.[45] A *reward* is anything an organism will work toward, and a *punisher* is anything that an organism will seek to avoid.[46] When a stimulus is perceived, it evokes an emotional state that causes an organism to perform a goal-oriented action coinciding with the reward or punisher perceived.[47] For example, fear could be the emotion evoked upon hearing a sound that is associated with electrical shock (punisher).[48] The perception of the punisher evokes the emotion of fear, which results in causing or motivating the organism to avoid the source of the sound.

Theories such as this conceive of emotions as the responses of an organism to its environment that are conducive to physical and social survival. For example, the expression of sorrow or sadness is thought to evoke

---

41. For examples of arguments supporting the distinction between pain and suffering, see Klein, *What the Body Commands*, 49–55.

42. See Klein, *What the Body Commands*, 186–88.

43. Martinez, "Imperative Content and the Painfulness of Pain," 76.

44. Klein, *What the Body Commands*, 188.

45. Rolls, *Emotion and Decision-Making Explained*, 14; see also Craig, "Interoception and Emotion," 272–74.

46. Rolls, *Emotion and Decision-Making Explained*, 14.

47. Rolls, *Emotion and Decision-Making Explained*, 16.

48. Rolls, *Emotion and Decision-Making Explained*, 15.

sympathetic and helping reactions from others in social settings.[49] In addition to the social benefits of sadness, in humans it is known to induce physiological responses that promote personal reflection.[50] Accordingly, it can result in an increase of attention to detail in the decision-making process.[51]

Of course, fear is a reaction to the environment that is necessary for survival. Fear occurs when an organism perceives a threat and is the emotion that promotes avoidance and escape.[52] Fear promotes two specific types of activity: defensive immobility (e.g., freezing and hyper-attentiveness) and defensive action (e.g., fight or flee).[53] In mammals, fear can be triggered not only by perceived physical threats, but also by perceived social threats.[54] Thus, fear is not only useful for physical survival, but also for social flourishing.

Anxiety has also been found to increase the survivability of nonhuman animals. This emotion is more complex than fear in that it involves possible future threats instead of present threats.[55] Researchers have found evidence of the advantages of anxiety in primates[56] and rodents[57] and, due to recent advances, believe that probably all vertebrates[58] and possibly invertebrates[59] benefit from anxiety.

Even depression and despair are thought to have functions conducive to survival. Several theories abound, and no consensus has been reached.

49. Bonanno et al., "Sadness and Grief," 799. See Keltner and Kring, "Emotion, Social Function, and Psychopathology," 324.

50. Bonanno et al., "Sadness and Grief," 799. See Lazarus, *Emotion and Adaptation*, 251.

51. Bonanno et al., "Sadness and Grief," 799. See Schwarz, "Warmer and More Social," 245.

52. Öhman and Mineka, "Fears, Phobias, and Preparedness," 483.

53. Lang et al., "Fear and Anxiety," 139.

54. Öhman and Mineka, "Fears, Phobias, and Preparedness," 486–87.

55. Perrot-Minnot et al., "Anxiety-Like Behaviour Increases Safety from Fish Predation," 2.

56. See Coleman and Pierre, "Assessing Anxiety in Nonhuman Primates," 333–46.

57. See Ganella and Kim, "Developmental Rodent Models of Fear and Anxiety," 4556–74.

58. See Stewart et al,. "Modeling Anxiety Using Adult Zebrafish," 135–43.

59. See Curran and Chlasani, "Serotonin Circuits and Anxiety," 81–92; Coleman and Pierre, "Assessing Anxiety in Nonhuman Primates," 333–46; Gibson et al., "Behavioral Responses to a Repetitive Visual Threat Stimulus," 1401–15; Hamilton et al., "Acute Fluoxetine Exposure Alters Crab Anxiety-Like Behaviour"; and Perrot-Minnot et al., "Anxiety-Like Behaviour Increases Safety from Fish Predation."

However, some have argued that depression promotes behaviors that minimize the risk of the loss of social connections and that also avoid the further loss of friends, family, goods, or opportunities.[60] A different theory is that depression is a defense mechanism that the body uses to promote behavior that protects a depressed person from infectious diseases.[61]

Is Animal Pain and Suffering Evil?

Given these contemporary theories of pain and suffering, alongside Aquinas's understandings of the same, it seems that the evil-as-privation theory does not face the complications that Kane and Robson emphasize. If pain, distress, fear, and despair are emotional states that are beneficial, then they cannot be viewed as evils. This is for at least two reasons. As mentioned above, one reason is they are physiological processes that occur in animals. According to Thomistic metaphysics, this means they are metaphysically good because they are actual; that is, they exist.[62]

A second reason they are not evils is because animals would be worse off without them.[63] It is no secret that pain is crucial for the well-being of complex organisms. Serge Marchand, neuroscientist and pain expert, explains,

> Pain is essential to survival. It plays an extremely important alarm role; in fact, it is our principal means of knowing that one of our organs is sick. For example, if we have appendicitis, the visceral pain becomes unbearable, which leads us to go to the doctor and get the necessary care. Without pain, we would have to wait for external signs such as a bump on the abdomen or even digestive or elimination problems. However, these signs generally come too late, when the infection has already spread throughout the body. . . .
>
> There are clinical cases of children born with a nervous system defect that makes them insensitive to pain (a congenital absence of the C fibers that are responsible for nociceptive transmission). These children, who experience virtually no pain, suffer significant wounds due to repeated injuries to the same area-fractures, joint injuries caused by poor posture when standing or walking, and even injuries to the tongue from biting it while chewing food. These children generally do not live very long, due to the fact that

---

60. Allen and Badcock, "Darwinian Models of Depression," 819.
61. Anders et al., "Depression as an Evolutionary Strategy," 9–22.
62. *ST* I, q. 5, a. 1; *De Veritate*, q. 21, a. 2.
63. For example, see Nagasako et al., "Congenital Insensitivity to Pain," 213–19.

they cannot detect the signs of an internal injury or pathology, which, without treatment, leads to fatal degeneration.[64]

Marchand emphasizes that, without pain, even seemingly small things, such as failing to shift when sitting or lying down, could cause physical problems.[65]

It also seems that emotions usually attributed with suffering are essential as well. Fear is certainly crucial for nonhuman animal survival. However, it seems that even sadness and depression increase the chances of nonhuman animal survival given the benefits of these emotional states mentioned above. Thus, emotions like pain, sorrow, fear, and despair are not only metaphysically good (in that they exist), but they also seem to be "natural and due" to nonhuman animals. This explains why Aquinas did not view them as privations of the good and why his understanding of emotions coheres with his theory of evil. There is no problem for the evil-as-privation theory because pain, sorrow, fear, and despair are good processes occurring in animals.

However, this does not mean there are no privations of the good entailed with unpleasant emotions. Aquinas discusses the privations associated with some of these emotions in his writings. For example, Aquinas mentions,

> A thing may be good or evil in two ways: first considered simply and in itself; and thus all sorrow is an evil, because the mere fact of a man's appetite being uneasy about a present evil, is itself an evil, because it hinders the response of the appetite in good.[66]

Here he is arguing that sorrow is considered an evil because it hinders an organism's response to its inclinations toward the good. In other words, pain and sadness can have adverse effects on an organism's ability to recognize and pursue what is good. For example, Aquinas mentions that pain can be so acute that it hinders human concentration and prevents learning.[67] Although unpleasant emotions serve a good purpose, they are involuntary processes that are absent from organisms in their normal state. They also oftentimes hinder the user-control of their subjects' thoughts, bodies, and actions. So, the privation of a good regarding the experience of pain and

---

64. Marchand, *Phenomenon of Pain*, 8.
65. Marchand, *Phenomenon of Pain*, 8.
66. ST I-II, q. 39, a. 1.
67. ST I-II, q. 37, a. 1.

suffering is that it entails an abnormal state of consciousness.[68] The privation of good in this abnormal state lies in that the suffering organism is not able to do things that it usually can do.[69]

This is another area of Aquinas's thought that is similar to contemporary scholarship. For example, Adam Swenson emphasizes that one bad aspect of pain is that it acts as a usurper upon its subject.[70] Pain is not only experienced as an unwelcome invader in the inner life of a subject, but it also seems to have an alien presence that is not a part of its subject.[71] In addition to the possible domination of the inner life of an organism, pain usurps the user control that organisms have over their thoughts, bodies, and actions.[72] It seems that this usurper concept also applies to unpleasant emotions, such as sadness, fear, and depression.

However, it is important to note that although there are absences of the good involved with unpleasant emotions, this does not cause problems for the evil-as-privation theory. The absence of the good involved with unpleasant emotions is a privation (and sometimes a perceived evil) from the perspective of the subject experiencing the emotions. However, pain and suffering are metaphysically good because they are natural and due to creatures. God has determined that humans and nonhuman animals possess these emotions because they are necessary for flourishing.

Therefore, to answer the question of whether pain and suffering are evils, they are not. Unpleasant emotions entail privations in that these emotions place organisms in an unwelcome state to which the organisms are unaccustomed. Unpleasant emotions also entail privations in that they usurp the user-control of their subjects. The alien nature of pain and suffering might seem like an evil from the perspective of the subject experiencing the emotions. Yet the unpleasant sensation and alien usurpation involved with these emotions are the very reason why they exist: to move their subject away from existing evils. Unpleasant emotions might seem evil to the subject experiencing them, but these emotions are metaphysically good and ensure the survival of their subject.

Usurpation and unpleasantness are certainly the aspects of pain and suffering that contribute to the assumption (without qualification) that

---

68. Anglin and Goetz, "Evil Is Privation," 5.
69. Anglin and Goetz, "Evil Is Privation," 7.
70. Swenson, "Pain's Evils," 208–16.
71. Swenson, "Pain's Evils," 210–11.
72. Swenson, "Pain's Evils," 208–9.

pain and suffering are evil. However, pain and suffering are metaphysically good in that they are actual, physiological processes that are beneficial to their subjects and in that they are natural to animals as determined by God. They are at all times natural and due to creatures. Without them, nonhuman animals would quickly die because they would not be motivated and/or involuntarily compelled to remove themselves from harm.

Evil as Privation and the Problem of Animal Suffering

This Thomistic interpretation of the evil-as-privation theory has important implications for the debate regarding the problem of animal suffering. As has been shown, it is often assumed that emotional states such as pain and suffering are evil. Theists themselves often assume that there needs to be an explanation for why God would allow for nonhuman animals to experience pain and suffering.

As mentioned in chapter 1, a few contemporary theists, labeled neo-Cartesians, have argued it is possible that nonhuman animals do not phenomenologically experience pain.[73] They do so because it is thought that if nonhuman animals are unaware of pains, then the problem of animal suffering is a non-starter. Indeed, a large amount of the literature regarding the problem of animal suffering involves the question of whether nonhuman animals phenomenologically experience pain like humans. However, even if nonhuman animals are not aware of their pains, there have been objections that neo-Cartesianism still fails to solve the problem of animal suffering.[74] Francescotti argues,

> the neo-Cartesian defenses do not satisfy Murray's standard of not conflicting with one's justified acceptances, and it seems that they also fail to meet the standard of not being significantly likely to be false. Another reason for rejecting the neo-Cartesian defenses (a point related to the issue of emotional suffering) is that these accounts focus only on the distress of *pain* while it is clear that there are phenomenally distressful mental states other than pain. Two obvious candidates are *depression* and *grief*, forms of emotional

---

73. For examples see Harrison, "Theodicy and Animal Pain," 79–92; Harrison, "Do Animals Feel Pain?," 25–40; and Murray, *Nature Red in Tooth and Claw*, 41–69.

74. For examples see Wennberg, "Animal Suffering and the Problem of Evil," 120–40; Lynch, "Harrison and Hick on God and Animal Pain," 63–68; and Francescotti, "Problem of Animal Pain and Suffering," 117–21.

suffering, which appear to be present in other mammals (seen especially in behavior exhibited at the death of kin).[75]

So Francescotti believes that theists need a much stronger answer to the problem of animal suffering than what has been proposed.[76]

However, the above considerations show that animal suffering does not pose the problem that it has been said to cause. Reconsider Rowe's argument: the fawn's suffering is assumed to be an evil that God should prevent unless it somehow brought about an equal or greater good. From a Thomistic perspective, the fawn's suffering is not an evil because it is a metaphysically good physiological process. If pain and suffering are not evil, then they are not things that God should be obligated to prevent without good reason as premises (1) and (2) of Rowe's argument suggest. Rowe's fawn may suffer for four days before it dies, but its suffering is natural and due to it. Without the ability to suffer and feel pain, the fawn may have never survived long enough to be caught in the forest fire. Thus, if pain and suffering are not evil, then God is not obligated to allow them only to bring about a greater good or prevent a lesser evil. There could even be instances of pointless nonhuman animal suffering, but it would be wrong to call such cases "evil." The fawn's suffering might not bring about a greater (or equal) good or prevent a worse (or equal) evil, but it is good in that it is serving its purpose of commanding the fawn to remove itself from the fire and the tree.

An objection to this conclusion might be that Aquinas has not avoided the problem. Some philosophers argue that evil-as-privation theories do not avoid the problem of evil, and instead they simply define the evil involved in the problem.[77] Perhaps along these lines, David Hume's criticism that there is no need for pain and suffering to be unpleasant would apply.[78] However, Murray has already emphasized that medical research has demonstrated this objection to fail.[79] In the late 1940s, surgeon Paul Brand worked with Hansen's disease (leprosy) patients with the goal, among others, of helping the needs of those patients who had lost the ability to feel pain in their hands and feet. Brand conducted a number of experiments aimed at warning the patients of physical dangers to their hands and feet.

---

75. Francescotti, "Problem of Animal Pain and Suffering," 120 (emphasis in original).

76. Francescotti, "Problem of Animal Pain and Suffering," 126.

77. For example see Ahern, "Note on the Nature of Evil," 17–25; and Ahern, "Nature of Evil," 35–44.

78. Hume, *Dialogues Concerning Natural Religion*, 11.5.

79. Murray, *Nature Red in Tooth and Claw*, 118–21.

All of these experiments ultimately failed to protect the patients from themselves and their environment. Brand recalls,

> We had grandly talked of retaining 'the good parts of pain without the bad,' which meant designing a warning system that would not hurt. First we tried a device like a hearing aid that would hum when the sensors were receiving normal pressures, buzz when they were in slight danger, and emit a piercing sound when they perceived an actual danger. But when a patient with a damaged hand turned a screwdriver too hard, the loud warning signal went off, he would simply override it . . . and turn the screwdriver anyway. Blinking lights failed for the same reason. Patients who perceived 'pain' only in the abstract could not be persuaded to trust artificial sensors. Or they became bored with the signals and ignored them. The sobering realization dawned on us that unless we built in a quality of compulsion, our substitute system would never work. Being alerted to the danger is not enough; our patient had to be forced to respond. Professor Tims of LSU said to me, almost in despair, 'Paul, it's no use. We'll never be able to protect these limbs unless the signal really hurts.' . . . We tried every alternative before resorting to pain, and finally concluded that Tims was right: the stimulus has to be unpleasant, just as pain is unpleasant.[80]

The unpleasantness involved with unpleasant emotions is necessary to compel their subjects to avoid the evil that is causing them to be experienced. Both humans and nonhuman animals would have no motivation to avoid damage to their bodies without the unpleasantness of pain and suffering.

Here it might be objected that although pain and suffering are not evils, it seems that God would not allow nonhuman animals to experience them in cases in which it seems they are not serving a purpose. For example, someone might object that an all-good, all-knowing, and all-powerful God would ensure that nonhuman animals quit feeling pain as soon as the pain serves no physiological purpose. They might say God would not allow Rowe's fawn to suffer after it was burned and injured to the point that it could not recover. Since it could not save itself, there was no need for pain. Objectors might also emphasize the seemingly pointless nature of conditions like chronic pain syndrome in nonhuman animals. Nonhuman animals can experience pain related to an injury long after the injury is gone (three to six months to qualify as chronic pain) and can eventually develop chronic pain syndrome in which they not only experience chronic

---

80. Yancey and Brand, *Gift of Pain*, 194.

pain, but also pain-related anxiety. Many other seemingly pointless cases exist, such as the pain and suffering associated with terminal cancer and other conditions.

At first, these might seem to be cases that leave the "evil" in "gratuitous evil" intact. However, it is good to reemphasize what is in question here; the main question under consideration in this chapter is not whether God has a reason for allowing evil (e.g., preventing another evil or bringing about another good), but whether pain and suffering are evil. Specifically, the question here is whether pointless pain and chronic pain syndrome can be understood as natural processes that God intends for animals. Another good thing to emphasize is that Rowe's argument is ultimately based in a logical problem posed by premises (1) and (2). It is not necessary to show that a solution to a logical problem is true. Instead it is only necessary that a solution to a logical problem be logically possible and avoid contradiction.

Many types of pain and suffering seem to have no point. For example, scientists still do not fully understand the mechanisms underlying chronic pain and how to treat it. Chronic pain has generally been thought to be maladaptive with no survival advantage for its subject (anxiety and increased pain are often associated with long-term pain[81]). However, in 2014, researchers discovered that long-term pain can be adaptive, at least in squid.[82] Squid are known to have the physiology necessary for nociceptive sensitization, a process in which repeated injury produces long-term pain because of an increasing sensitivity to pain and even spontaneous pain sensations in the injured areas.[83] Regarding this sensitization, a team of researchers found that repeatedly-injured squid initiated defensive behaviors earlier than non-injured squid when being pursued by black sea bass (a natural fish predator).[84] They concluded that, although injured squid were pursued more by predators, the injured squid were able to respond to predators better due to their increased sensitivity to pain. While chronic pain may seem maladaptive, it can serve a purpose. Thus, it does not seem difficult to imagine that there are good physiological reasons for other types of seemingly purposeless types of pain and suffering.

81. Melzack and Wall, *Challenge of Pain*, 36.
82. Crook et al., "Nociceptive Sensitization Reduces Predation Risk," 1121–25.
83. See Crook et al., "Squid Have Nociceptors that Display Widespread Long-Term Sensitization," 10021–26.
84. Crook et al., "Nociceptive Sensitization Reduces Predation Risk."

The Nature of Animal Suffering and God's Goodness

Regarding the problem of physiological pointless pain, there could be practical reasons why God would not install a "kill switch" system in animals so they would quit feeling pain when it will no longer help them. For one, physiological systems do not work as well when animals age. It is logically possible that God does not intend for animals to quit feeling pain when it is unnecessary because a pain kill-switch system might fail in old age and cause older animals to die prematurely. Moreover, the kill switch would need to activate at particular moments and be set off by particular stimuli. But it is not clear what these would be. Should the fawns quit feeling pain when they experience a large impact such as a tree falling on them? If so, a fawn might stop feeling pain after accidentally ramming into another fawn. Such an incident could cause the fawn that now cannot feel pain to quickly injure itself. Should the fawn quit feeling pain after a certain duration or intensity of pain? If so, a fawn might stop feeling pain when it has a broken leg that takes longer to heal. Yet such an injury would never heal if the fawn quit feeling pain.

It seems that any species with any type of physiological pain kill-switch system would be at an evolutionary disadvantage. Animals that prematurely stop feeling pain due to an improper activation of their kill switch or due to an aging or malfunctioning kill switch would die off, leaving only those animals that are constantly able to feel pain. It is logically possible that the nonhuman animal ability to feel pain even in terminal situations is a design tradeoff that helps them survive in a world with fixed physical laws, especially since nonhuman animals are guided by instincts and limited animal intelligence.

Thus, premises (1) and (2) of Rowe's argument are false because nonhuman animal suffering is not evil, even if suffering will not save the life of its subject. Premise (1) is false because nonhuman animal suffering is not evil and does not require a moral explanation involving the prevention of evils or the production of goods. Premise (2) is false for a similar reason in that God would not necessarily prevent intense suffering because of a moral obligation to produce a greater good or prevent a greater evil. This entails that no number of cases of animal pain and suffering, even pointless nonhuman animal pain and suffering, will amount to evidence against God. Yet, if this is not compelling enough, more can be said regarding premise (2).

Considering God's Goodness and Moral Obligations

Premise (2) of Rowe's argument involves the idea that God is obligated to eliminate evils (such as intense suffering, which is assumed to be evil) unless God is allowing them for a good reason. If God allowed intense suffering without the suffering bringing about a greater (or equal) good or preventing a greater (or equal) evil, then it would be concluded that God is not wholly good. As mentioned, much of the debate over Rowe's argument has involved premise (2).

In what follows, it will be shown that Aquinas would disagree with premise (2). Aquinas argues that from what we know about God from the Five Ways, we can know that God is infinite goodness.[85] When Aquinas says that God is "good," he means something different from what is usually meant today when it is said that humans are "good." However, before explaining Aquinas's thought regarding God's goodness, it is necessary to understand Aquinas's concept of the good.

The Thomistic Concept of God's Goodness

Expanding on Aristotle, Aquinas believes that *goodness* and *being* are interchangeable concepts in that something is good insofar as it is a perfect example of its kind:

> Goodness and being are really the same, and differ only in idea; which is clear from the following argument. The essence of goodness consists in this, that it is in some way desirable. Hence the Philosopher says (*Ethic.* i.): *Goodness is what all desire.* Now it is clear that a thing is desirable only in so far as it is perfect; for all desire their own perfection. But everything is perfect so far as it is actual. Therefore it is clear that a thing is perfect so far as it exists; for it is existence that makes all things actual, as is clear from the foregoing (Q. 3, A. 4; Q. 4, A. 1). Hence it is clear that goodness and being are the same really.[86]

Aquinas here is assuming his readers understand the Scholastic concept of final causes. The good is "appetible" in the sense that all things tend toward the perfection of their natures as far as they can. For example, nonhuman animals work constantly to keep themselves healthy and to survive as long

---

85. See *ST* I, q. 6.
86. *ST* I, q. 5, a. 1.

The Nature of Animal Suffering and God's Goodness

as possible. Human beings constantly work not only to stay healthy, but also to accumulate wealth, knowledge, power, and other things they deem will give them happiness and fulfillment. Even organisms that lack self-awareness and consciousness act in a manner so that they obtain the perfection of their natures, unless they are impeded. For example, acorns always grow into oak trees (if unimpeded) although they do not have minds and cannot know how to obtain their perfection. Basically, using Aristotle's definition of *good* as "that what all desire," Aquinas is saying that since things desire (or tend toward) their perfection, and since something is only perfect insofar as it exists as an ideal instance of its kind, being is interchangeable with goodness.

With Aquinas's concept of goodness in mind, his Five Ways lead to the conclusion that God is infinite goodness. This conclusion follows because Aquinas's Five Ways entail that God is pure actuality with no potentiality;[87] God is existence itself in that God's essence is existence;[88] and God is infinitely perfect, infinite being, and the source of all perfections in the universe.[89] If goodness is being as far as it is desirable, and God is infinite being, it follows that God is infinite goodness and infinitely desirable.[90] Also, if beings are good insofar as they are ideal instances of their kind, and God is infinitely perfect, it follows that God is infinite goodness.[91]

Aquinas argues that God's perfection and infinite goodness have implications for which virtues God can possess. For example, Aquinas says,

> the divine goodness contains in its own way all virtues. Therefore, none of them is ascribed as a habit to God as it is to us. For it is not befitting God to be good through something else added to him, but by his essence, for he is altogether simple. Nor does he act by anything added to his essence, since his action is his being, as we have shown. Therefore, his virtue is not a habit, but his essence.[92]

As the source of the eternal and natural laws, all virtues are eminently in God. Humans are understood as virtuous insofar as they cultivate virtuous habits that help them attain their perfection. But God does not need to obtain virtuous habits because God is infinitely perfect.

87. *ST* I, q. 3, a. 2; *SCG* I, c. 16.
88. *ST* I, q. 3, a. 4; *SCG* I, c. 21; see *De ente*.
89. *ST* I, q. 4, a. 1; *SCG* I, c. 28.
90. *ST* I, q. 6, a. 1; *SCG* I, c. 37.
91. *ST* I, q. 6, a. 3; *SCG* I, c. 38.
92. *SCG* I, c. 92.

Although God is the source of all human virtues, Aquinas says that many virtues cannot be found in God, such as sobriety and chastity, because God does not eat, drink, or have sex.[93] Also, fortitude is not a virtue in God because God can never face dangers. However, Aquinas believes God can be virtuous in terms of truth, justice, liberality, magnificence, prudence, and art.[94] For example, Aquinas believes there is perfect distributive justice in God because in creating and sustaining the universe, God determines the good of each of God's creatures and ensures they possess exactly what God determined.[95] Also, Aquinas thinks that God's act of creating and sustaining the universe is an act of liberality and love.[96] It is liberal because God is infinitely perfect and in no need of creating anything. It is loving because *to love* is to "will the good of the beloved." God's pure act is an act of love because in creating and sustaining the universe, God is willing the good (i.e., the existence and perfection) of each of his creatures.

Although Aquinas believes that God has virtue in some ways, Aquinas would not agree that this leads to comprehensive knowledge of how God should act.[97] Aquinas argues that we can never fully understand God because God is infinite and invisible. In regard to the epistemological implications of God's infinity, Aquinas says,

> Everything is knowable according to its actuality. But God, whose being is infinite, as was shown above (Q. 7), is infinitely knowable. Now no created intellect can know God infinitely. For the created intellect knows the divine essence more or less perfectly in proportion as it receives a greater or lesser light of glory. Since therefore the created light of glory received into any created intellect cannot be infinite, it is clearly impossible for any created intellect to know God in an infinite degree. Hence it is impossible that it should comprehend God.[98]

Regarding the implications of God's invisibility, he argues,

---

93. *SCG* I, c. 92.
94. *SCG* I, c. 93.
95. *SCG* I, c. 93; see also *ST* I, q. 21, a. 1.
96. *SCG* I, c. 91, 93; see also *ST* I, q. 20, a. 2.
97. Thomist Brian Davies has also argued that Aquinas's philosophy entails that God should not be understood as morally perfect in the same way humans are. See Davies, *Reality of God and the Problem of Evil*, 84–111; and Davies, *Thomas Aquinas on God and Evil*, 51–64.
98. *ST* I, q. 12, a. 7; see *SCG* III, c. 52.

> God cannot be seen in His essence by a mere human being, except he be separated from this mortal life. The reason, is because, as was said above (A. 4), the mode of knowledge follows the mode of the nature of the knower. But our soul, as long as we live in this life, has its being in corporeal matter; hence naturally it knows only what has a form in matter, or what can be known by such a form. Now it is evident that the Divine essence cannot be known through the nature of material things. For it was shown above (AA. 2, 9) that the knowledge of God by means of any created similitude is not the vision of His essence. Hence it is impossible for the soul of man in this life to see the essence of God.[99]

Moreover, we can only have analogical knowledge of God because God is transcendent, and all we know of him comes from reasoning from his effects to him as the cause:

> Our natural knowledge begins from sense. Hence our natural knowledge can go as far as it can be led by sensible things. But our mind cannot be led by sense so far as to see the essence of God; because the sensible effects of God do not equal the power of God as their cause. Hence from the knowledge of sensible things the whole power of God cannot be known; nor therefore can His essence be seen. But because they are His effects and depend on their cause, we can be led from them so far as to know of God *whether He exists*, and to know of Him what must necessarily belong to Him, as the first cause of all things, exceeding all things caused by Him.[100]

To know how God will act in any given situation, it would be necessary to fully understand God's infinite goodness, which is impossible.

Thus, Aquinas would agree that the term *good* does not mean exactly the same thing when applied to God and to humans. Although we cannot know how God will act, we can know some things about what it means for God to be infinite goodness: God is infinite being, infinitely desirable, loving, and just; humans are good insofar as they act virtuously and attain their perfection; and goodness is attributed to God and to humans analogously.

---

99. *ST* I, q. 12, a. 11.
100. *ST* I, q. 12, a. 12; see also *SCG* I, c. 34.

Thomism and the Problem of Animal Suffering

God's Goodness and the Problem of Animal Suffering

Returning to the problem of animal suffering, it should now be apparent why Aquinas's concept of God's goodness is pertinent to Rowe's premise (2). When God and humans are said to be "good" in classical theism, this is not meant univocally. God is thought of as just and loving because he wills the good of his creatures at every moment they exist and guides them to him as their ultimate end. The notion that God ought to only allow intense suffering if it brings about a greater (or equal) good or prevents a greater (or equal) evil is unprovable because we are not in the position to know how God ought to act.

This Thomistic understanding of God's goodness is not the same as skeptical theism. Skeptical theists hold that we cannot know why God would allow evils in any given situation because we do not have epistemic access to God's infinite knowledge and wisdom. However, skeptical theism assumes that God should eliminate evil unless he has a good reason for allowing it. This Thomistic understanding of God's goodness does not assume to know what God should or should not do. Since we cannot know God's infinite goodness and how God should act, we cannot say that God *should* eliminate evil, and the occurrence of evil is not evidence against his existence. Thus, the truth of premise (2) of Rowe's argument cannot be known, and it cannot provide a basis for an argument against the God of classical theism.

Conclusion

The problem of animal suffering, as it was formulated by Rowe in "The Problem of Evil and Some Varieties of Atheism," does not stand against classical theism. As shown, it is wrong to assume that nonhuman animal suffering is an evil that God is obligated to prevent or an evil that God should only allow for good reason. Regarding premise (1) of Rowe's argument, from a Thomistic perspective, animal pain and suffering are found to be metaphysically good in that unpleasant emotions are physiological processes that exist to help nonhuman animals to survive and flourish in a world governed by physical laws. Even intense nonhuman animal suffering that seems to be maladaptive has been found to improve the survivability of nonhuman animals. Some instances of intense nonhuman animal suffering might not result in survival for nonhuman animals, but it is possible that

The Nature of Animal Suffering and God's Goodness

this is a design tradeoff that maximizes nonhuman animal flourishing in a world governed by physical laws.

Regarding premise (2) of Rowe's argument, from a Thomistic perspective, it is not certain that God should prevent intense nonhuman animal suffering unless the suffering brings about a greater (or equal) good or prevents a greater (or equal) evil. For one, it was shown that intense nonhuman animal suffering is not evil. But just as important, from a Thomistic perspective, it can be known that God exists and is infinite goodness. God is infinite existence, and since the good is that what all desire, God is infinitely desirable and infinitely good. Since God is the source of all goodness in the world, all human virtues are eminently in God. However, because God is infinitely perfect, many human virtues cannot be predicated of God, such as sobriety, chastity, and fortitude, while some can, such as truth, justice, liberality, etc. While much can be known about God in this life, how God ought to act in many specific situations is unknowable because it would require knowing God's infinite essence, which is impossible. Thus, it cannot be known whether God should only allow intense suffering if it brings about a greater (or equal) good or prevents a greater (or equal) evil.

These Thomistic concepts are sufficient to refute Rowe's argument, although some people might not find them compelling. A question that might remain concerns why God would make a world with contingent creatures susceptible to suffering and death in which it is necessary to make design tradeoffs. This question will be answered in chapter 4 when Paul Draper's inference-to-the-best-explanation argument is discussed. Another issue that might remain involves God's goodness in relation to his omnipotence. Some might argue that God should not allow nonhuman animals to suffer regardless of whether nonhuman animal suffering is good for them. Suffering is unpleasant, and a loving and all-powerful God has the ability to keep his creatures from all suffering. To answer this objection, and to build on the case against Rowe's evidential argument, the next chapter will discuss the nature of the nonhuman animal soul.

3

The Nature of the Animal Soul[1]

ONE QUESTION REMAINING IS whether an infinitely powerful and loving God would allow nonhuman animal suffering. Regardless of whether intense nonhuman animal suffering is good or whether it contributes to nonhuman animal flourishing, suffering is still unpleasant. So, if God is all-powerful and all-loving, then should not God make a world where nonhuman animals are kept from suffering or at least a world in which there is less nonhuman animal suffering? Even if suffering is metaphysically good, is there not a moral issue with God allowing nonhuman animals to experience pain and suffering against their will? Answers to these questions can be found when considering the nature of the nonhuman animal soul.

As mentioned in chapter 1, some philosophers, called neo-Cartesians, have thought it possible that nonhuman animals do not phenomenologically experience pain. In other words, neo-Cartesians believe that nonhuman animals are philosophical zombies: beings that look like they possess consciousness but are not conscious of anything, or at least are not conscious of pain. Neo-Cartesianism is obviously significant regarding the problem of animal suffering because if nonhuman animals do not phenomenologically experience pain, then there is no problem of animal suffering. Regarding William Rowe's evidential argument, if neo-Cartesianism is true, then premise (1) is false because no instances of intense suffering would exist at all. However, few scholars have found the neo-Cartesian position compelling.[2] As mentioned, many philosophers, including theists, have argued

---

1. Almost in its entirety, this chapter was taken from Keltz, "Neo-Thomism and the Problem of Animal Suffering," 93–125.

2. Out of eight scholarly reviews of *Nature Red in Tooth and Claw* I found, only

that neo-Cartesian arguments fail and that the problem of animal suffering still stands.[3] So, although there have been a few other major attempts at defending theism from the problem of animal suffering (as discussed in chapter 1), it seems that theists have not been successful at providing compelling arguments from nonhuman animal consciousness against the problem of animal suffering.

With this situation in mind, as mentioned, this chapter attempts to provide a solution to the problem of animal suffering similar to Murray and Ross's neo-Cartesian arguments. First, I will briefly discuss the four neo-Cartesian positions regarding nonhuman animal minds and how they attempt to avoid the problem of animal suffering. These positions will help provide a contrast when I next describe Aquinas's positions regarding animal souls and human self-awareness. After describing the neo-Cartesian and Thomistic positions, I will discuss contemporary philosophical and scientific viewpoints regarding nonhuman animal rationality, metacognition, and episodic memory. The contemporary evidence will help me to propose a neo-Thomistic view of nonhuman animal minds in relation to the problem of animal suffering. After considering an objection, I will conclude that the neo-Thomistic view provides a more compelling alternative to the neo-Cartesian solution to the problem of animal suffering, especially as it is formulated by Rowe.

Nonhuman Animal Minds and the Problem of Animal Suffering

Neo-Cartesianism

As mentioned, the neo-Cartesian answer to the problem of animal suffering is to deny that nonhuman animals are aware of any pain. Again, Murray and Ross list four neo-Cartesian options regarding nonhuman animals and pain:

---

one was positive (Mawson, review of *Nature Red in Tooth and Claw*, 855–58). The others were either neutral, said Murray's arguments will not compel most readers, or were downright hostile to Murray's arguments. Also, see below where I emphasize that even the major opponents to the problem of animal suffering argue against Murray.

3. For examples see Creegan, *Animal Suffering and the Problem of Evil*, 31–32, 51–53; Francescotti, "Problem of Animal Pain and Suffering," 114–21; and Dougherty, *Problem of Animal Pain*, 56–95.

Thomism and the Problem of Animal Suffering

1. Many nonhuman creatures are conscious inasmuch as they are alive, awake and have sensations.... Yet, unlike the sensory states possessed by humans, the mechanisms whereby these organisms have access to the world lack any phenomenal character whatsoever;[4]

2. For a mental state to be a conscious state (phenomenally) requires an accompanying higher-order mental state (a HOT) that has that state as its intentional object.... Only humans have the cognitive faculties required to form the conception of themselves being in a first-order state that one must have in order to have a HOT;[5]

3. Some nonhuman creatures have states that have intrinsic phenomenal qualities analogous to those possessed by humans when they are in states of pain. These creatures lack, however, any higher-order states of being aware of themselves as being in first-order states;[6] and

4. Most creatures lack the cognitive faculties required to be in a higher-order state of recognizing themselves to be in a first-order state of pain. Those nonhuman creatures that can on occasion achieve a second-order access to their first-order states of pain, nonetheless do not have the capacity to regard that second-order state as undesirable.[7]

As mentioned, these options entail that nonhuman animals either (1) lack phenomenal consciousness, (2) lack the higher-order mental states required for phenomenal consciousness, (3) are phenomenally conscious of pain but lack higher-order mental states, or (4) are phenomenally aware of pain, and some have higher-order mental states regarding the pain, but lack the capacity to regard such higher states as undesirable. If one of these options were found to be true, then the problem of animal suffering would dissolve.

These four possible options are called neo-Cartesian because they draw inspiration from the writings of René Descartes. As mentioned in chapter 1, Descartes's philosophy entails that the immaterial mind/soul provides humans with the capacity for conscious mental states.[8] Thus, if nonhuman animals do not demonstrate the capacity for rational thought, then it seems

---

4. Murray and Ross, "Neo-Cartesianism and the Problem of Animal Suffering," 175.
5. Murray and Ross, "Neo-Cartesianism and the Problem of Animal Suffering," 176.
6. Murray and Ross, "Neo-Cartesianism and the Problem of Animal Suffering," 176.
7. Murray and Ross, "Neo-Cartesianism and the Problem of Animal Suffering," 177.
8. Descartes, *Discourse on Method*, 4.

they would lack both minds/souls and phenomenal consciousness.[9] These four neo-Cartesian positions emphasize that there is no evidence necessitating the conclusion that nonhuman animals possess phenomenal consciousness. Thus, they conclude that God's nonexistence does not necessarily follow from the appearance of nonhuman animal suffering.

Thomism and the Nonhuman Animal Soul

Thomas Aquinas is also infamous for his position regarding nonhuman animal minds. Following Aristotle, Aquinas believed that humans possess rational souls, while nonhuman animals merely possess sensitive souls.[10] Humans are capable of consciousness and movement as are other animals, but humans are the only animals with the abilities of the intellect and will. This crucial difference entails that nonhuman animals lack the ability to understand what they experience and are unable to act rationally. For example, Aquinas says,

> Now we cannot find in the souls of dumb animals any operation superior to those of the sensitive part, for they neither understand nor reason. This appears from the fact that all animals of the same species operate in the same way, as though moved by nature and not as operating by art: thus every swallow builds its nest, and every spider spins its web, in the same way. Therefore, the souls of dumb animals have no operation that is possible without the body.[11]

As will be discussed below, the nonhuman animal lack of an intellect and will entails that they are neither moral agents nor is their suffering morally significant.

Aquinas's position might seem to be very close to the Cartesian position.[12] Indeed, Cartesianism and Thomism are similar in that rationality

---

9. As mentioned in chapter 1, some of Descartes's writings indicate that his mature view regarding animals was closer to the Aristotelian/Thomistic view than the view that many attribute to him (see Steiner, "Descartes, Christianity, and Contemporary Speciesism," 118–23; and Cottingham, "Descartes' Treatment of Animals," 225–33). However, much of his philosophy entails that animals lack phenomenal consciousness.

10. For example, see *SCG* II, c. 60.

11. *SCG* II, c. 82.

12. Regardless of the debate over Descartes's position regarding animals, for sake of ease, I will use the terms *Cartesian position* and *Cartesianism* to refer to the view often attributed to Descartes entailing that animals lack phenomenal consciousness because they lack immaterial minds/souls.

serves as a criterion for moral agency and personhood. However, there are significant differences between the two positions. Cartesianism includes the idea that the mind/soul is what gives humans the ability to possess consciousness and rationality. Nonhuman animals are thought to be alive, but arational and nonconscious. This, of course, is why neo-Cartesianism is mainly concerned with determining to what degree nonhuman animals possess phenomenal consciousness. Thomism holds that the soul is the principle of life in biological organisms and is that which distinguishes life from non-life. There are different types of souls (i.e., vegetative, sensitive, and rational), which possess different types of abilities (e.g., reproduction, movement, rationality, etc.).

For Cartesianism, testing for rationality in nonhuman animals is only one way for trying to determine if they are conscious. If they show signs of phenomenal consciousness, then they necessarily possess a mind/soul and are rational. So neo-Cartesianism is mainly concerned with whether nonhuman animals have any degree of phenomenal consciousness, not necessarily whether they exhibit human levels of rationality. For Thomism, testing for rationality and self-consciousness are the main ways to determine if animals are persons capable of moral agency. This is because, following Aquinas, consciousness is necessary to explain many animal behaviors. Aquinas explains,

> For the type of every act or operation is determined by an object. Every operation of the soul is the act of a potentiality—either active or passive. Now the objects of passive potentialities stand to these as the causal agents which bring each potentiality into its proper activity; and it is thus that visible objects, and indeed all sensible things, are related to sight and to the other senses.[13]

Here he is mentioning that objects in nature act on the passive senses of organisms. If an organism reacts to sights, sounds, smells, etc., it is inferred that such an organism possesses the sense or senses that explain such behavior. Aquinas was not concerned with "what it is like" to be an organism, but only whether an organism possesses the ability to sense its environment. John Haldane helps to explain this further:

> There is an old Aristotelian principle according to which acts are distinguished by their respective objects, powers are known by their acts, and substances are defined by their powers.... What is of prime importance in determining if an individual is sensate

13. *In De Anima* II, lec. 6, n. 305.

is not the question of what it is like to be it, or even whether that Nagelian question arises; but rather the issue of how the individual is related to its environment. We do not need telepathy in order to attribute sensory awareness, for perception shows itself in the eye of the perceiver—*vultus est index animi*. On this basis there can be no serious doubt that dogs see other dogs.[14]

As Haldane suggests, Thomism does not entail a skepticism toward nonhuman animal consciousness as does neo-Cartesianism. If an organism reacts to its environment, it is assumed that the organism is conscious of that to which it reacts.

Aquinas on Reasoning and Self-Knowledge

To Thomists, rationality and self-awareness are the main criteria for moral agency and personhood for two major reasons. One reason is the intellect and will are thought to be immaterial, making it possible for rational animals to possess free will. The other reason is that Aquinas's theory of self-knowledge entails animals without intellects cannot be self-aware. To better understand these concepts, it will be good to discuss them further and draw out their implications for personhood.

Reasoning

The Aristotelian/Thomistic concept of reasoning sometimes gets confused in the contemporary discussion regarding nonhuman animal minds.[15] Indeed, the term *rational* can have different meanings depending on the discipline of the person using it. For example, Alex Kacelnik has emphasized that there are at least three different meanings of *rational* used across the disciplines of philosophy, psychology, economics, and biology.[16] Thus, it is crucial to be clear on the meaning of this term as understood in Thomism.

Following the Islamic philosopher Avicenna, Aquinas believed that nonhuman animals possess an estimative power. This power allows them

---

14. Haldane, *Reasonable Faith*, 122–23.

15. Matthew Boyle provides a discussion of the Aristotelian understanding of reasoning in light of recent findings in philosophy and science, although his discussion is light on explaining Aristotle's view of human reasoning. See Boyle, "Different Kind of Mind?," 109–18.

16. Kacelnik, "Meanings of Rationality," 87–106.

to recognize intentions that are not directly perceived by their senses.[17] The estimative power is similar to animal survival instincts and, among other things, recognizes whether something is useful or harmful to the animal perceiving.[18] This power involves nonhuman animals processing and reacting to sense data they perceive and resembles empirical induction.

While nonhuman animals only appear to use logical reasoning because of their estimative power, rational animals (i.e., humans) are able to reason because they possess immaterial intellects. For example, in a simple syllogism, there are both universal and particular concepts involved. The intellect is necessary to know and understand the universal statement, "All men are mortal." The senses are necessary to observe the particular statement, "Socrates is a man." The intellect concludes that "Socrates is mortal" based on the relation between the particular Socrates (who is judged to be a man) and the universal concept of humanity (which is known to include mortality). Without the intellect, it would be impossible to know universal concepts because universal concepts are immaterial.[19] When forms (containing universals) are conjoined with matter, they become particular instances of themselves. But observing a particular human will never give full knowledge of humanity. It is only when the universal and immaterial concept of humanity is abstracted from the form of a particular human and stored in the immaterial intellect that knowledge of humanity is possible.

Thus, Aquinas believed that nonhuman animals were not capable of complex, abstract reasoning. Nonhuman animals are completely physical and do not possess immaterial intellects;[20] they are unable to *know* universal forms and make judgments based on these forms and their relations. All they are able to do is observe particulars and react to their observations through their estimative powers.[21]

---

17. *ST* I, q. 78, a. 4; *De anima*, a. 13.
18. Stump, *Aquinas*, 258.
19. See *ST* I, q. 75, a. 5; *De Veritate*, q. 10, a. 8.
20. *SCG* II, c. 82.
21. This would not qualify as rationality for Aquinas but is similar to the understanding of rationality in biology, which understands *rationality* as performing actions that are conducive to fitness. See Kacelnik, "Meanings of Rationality," 87–106.

The Nature of the Animal Soul
Self-Knowledge

Besides reasoning, Aquinas believed that the immaterial intellect made it possible for rational animals to possess self-knowledge. The intellect makes this possible in two distinct ways: the self can be known through philosophical argumentation and also through the act of understanding.[22] The latter way is the most important for the current discussion.

The intellect, according to Aquinas, is composed of two distinct powers: the passive intellect and the active intellect.[23] Aquinas believed that when the active intellect abstracts a form and deposits it into the passive intellect, the knower not only knows the form, but also knows that he is knowing.[24] So in the act of knowing, the mind perceives itself. This is intuitive self-knowledge because this knowledge of the self is gained through direct cognition, as opposed to the discursive reasoning involved in philosophical argumentation.[25]

Aquinas says that in the act of knowing, the intellect judges that there is an "I" that is distinct from the object that is known.[26] This is because the intellect not only knows, but knows that it knows as it gains knowledge. The knower cognizes objects as objects that are known by a knower, an "I," and this creates an intuitive subject/object relation between knower and thing known.[27]

When the "I" is perceived in the act of knowing, the intellect judges that the "I" exists.[28] Aquinas believed that when the intellect cognizes something, it judges that the thing exists.[29] Thus, if the intellect cognizes an "I" in the process of knowing, it also judges that the "I" exists.[30] Over time, this awareness of an "I" produces a diachronic unity of consciousness in that it is known that the same "I" remains throughout all experiences.[31]

---

22. Cory, *Aquinas on Human Self-Knowledge*, 63–64. See *ST* I, q. 87, a. 1; *De Veritate*, q. 10, a. 8.

23. *ST* I, q. 79, a. 2–3; *De anima*, a. 4.

24. *ST* I, q. 87, a. 3; q. 93, a. 7, ad4; *SCG* III, c. 46.

25. For an in-depth treatment of this process of intuitive self-awareness, see Cory, *Aquinas on Human Self-Knowledge*, 69–133.

26. Cory, *Aquinas on Human Self-Knowledge*, 84.

27. Cory, *Aquinas on Human Self-Knowledge*, 204.

28. Cory, *Aquinas on Human Self-Knowledge*, 84.

29. *De Veritate*, q. 10, a. 8.

30. Cory, *Aquinas on Human Self-Knowledge*, 84.

31. Cory, *Aquinas on Human Self-Knowledge*, 207.

Nonhuman animals are thought to lack self-awareness because they are unable to perform the acts of the mind like simple apprehension and reasoning. They can sense and remember things, but this only happens on the level of particulars. Their lack of an immaterial intellect renders them incapable of storing universal concepts. Accordingly, they do not experience the act of knowing like rational animals do.

Contemporary Theories Regarding Rationality and Self-Consciousness

In light of the discussion on Aquinas's position, it will be good to review contemporary research regarding nonhuman animal minds. Since Thomists doubt the existence of abstract reasoning and self-awareness in nonhuman animals, I will only discuss contemporary research regarding these concepts. So, in what follows, I will focus on contemporary findings regarding nonhuman animal rationality, metacognition, and episodic memory.

Abstract Reasoning

As mentioned, research into nonhuman animal rationality can be confusing because of the many different uses of the term *rationality*. However, there has been plenty of contemporary research conducted on the specific type of abstract reasoning that Thomism entails. The literature on nonhuman animal rationality is massive, and space precludes a proper review. Thus, I will emphasize only the most relevant theories and their objections.

There are many researchers who believe there is evidence suggesting that some nonhuman animals are capable of various types of logical inferences including exclusionary inferences (great apes and dogs[32]), transitive inferences (monkeys, baboons, and sea lions[33]), and causal inferences (apes,

---

32. For examples see Call, "Descartes' Two Errors," 219–34; Call, "Inferences by Exclusion in the Great Apes," 393–403; and Erdőhegyi et al., "Dog-Logic," 725–37.

33. For examples see McGonigle and Chalmers, "Are Monkeys Logical?," 694–96; McGonigle and Chalmers, "Monkeys Are Rational!," 198–228; Schusterman et al., "Cognitive Sea Lion," 217–28; and Seyfarth and Cheney, "Structure of Social Knowledge in Monkeys," 379–84.

monkeys, and rats[34]).[35] For example, in an experiment involving several different breeds, researchers tested for the existence of the ability for exclusionary inference in dogs.[36] The tests involved a ball and two containers. In the tests, an experimenter would call the dog, show the dog a ball, and place the ball under one of the identical containers in a way so that the dog could not see the location of the ball. Afterward, the experimenter would provide the dog with information regarding the location of the ball by either lifting both containers, the empty container, or the container with the ball. The dog was then allowed to attempt to find the ball for a reward. A second version of the tests involved the lifting of the containers by strings without an experimenter present. The tests revealed that the dogs performed significantly higher than chance results and led the researchers to conclude that dogs are able to perform exclusionary inferences.[37]

However, there is no consensus on the issue of abstract rationality in nonhuman animals as its existence is doubted by other researchers.[38] For example, José Bermúdez argues it is possible that nonhuman animals are not using the same kind of abstract logic, similar to humans, but are instead using a type of proto-logic.[39] Bermúdez believes that nonhuman animals are unable to perform abstract reasoning without language.[40] Since nonhuman animals can only think nonlinguistically, they are unable to make truth judgments regarding their thoughts because they lack the means to label their thoughts as true or false.

This lack would entail that the dogs were not performing an exclusionary inference such as:

1. Either the ball is in container A or the ball is in container B.
2. It is not true that the ball is in container A.

---

34. For examples see Dickinson and Shanks, "Instrumental Action and Causal Representation," 5–25; Call, "Descartes' Two Errors," 219, 234; Blaisdell et al., "Causal Reasoning in Rats," 1020–22; and Hauser and Santos, "Evolutionary Ancestry of Our Knowledge of Tools," 267–88.

35. Beck, "Do Animals Engage in Conceptual Thought?," 225–26.

36. Erdőhegyi et al., "Dog-Logic," 725–37.

37. Erdőhegyi et al., "Dog-Logic," 734–35.

38. For examples see Bermúdez, *Thinking Without Words*, 109–32; Penn and Povinelli, "Causal Cognition in Human and Nonhuman Animals," 97–118; and Penn et al., "Darwin's Mistake," 109–30.

39. Bermúdez, "Animal Reasoning and Proto-Logic," 127–38.

40. See Bermúdez, "Can Nonlinguistic Animals Think about Thinking?," 119–30.

3. Therefore, it is true that the ball is in container B.

Instead, they would perform a proto-logical process similar to:

1. The ball is absent from container A.
2. The ball is in container B.

Without the ability to form thoughts about thoughts, such as "Either A or B," the dogs would be unable to formulate the proposition that establishes a disjunctive syllogism. Furthermore, if they were able to establish the first proposition, they would be unable to formulate a truth-conditional thought, such as, "It is not true that A," so as to guarantee the truth of the conclusion. Instead, utilizing a type of proto-logic, the dogs would be able to quickly learn to associate two subcontraries: "The ball is absent from container A" is associated with "The ball is in container B."

Thus, it could appear that the dogs use exclusionary inferences, when in fact they are simply associating subcontraries. They may not consider abstract logical relations, but merely perform the action that usually leads to a reward upon observing the absence of the ball in one of two containers. Their actions appear logical, but the process that determines their actions is not based on logic and does not produce necessarily valid conclusions.

Regarding the other types of reasoning, researchers have proposed ways in which it is possible that animals appear to use abstract reasoning, but do not.[41] For example, in addition to Bermúdez's proposal, Michael Rescorla suggests it is possible that the appearance of exclusionary inferences can be explained by a process of Bayesian updating over cognitive maps.[42] Associative learning and/or innate biases are also thought to provide an explanation for the appearance of transitive and causal inferences.[43]

Alongside this debate, there is a major position in the field of psychology called dual-system theory, which is pertinent to the current discussion. Dual-system theorists hold that there are two distinct reasoning systems involved in human cognition.[44] One system, known as System 1, involves

---

41. Beck, "Do Animals Engage in Conceptual Thought?," 226.

42. Rescorla, "Cognitive Maps and the Language of Thought," 377–407.

43. Zentall, "Case for a Cognitive Approach to Animal Learning and Behavior," 65–78; De Lillo et al., "Transitive Choices by a Simple, Fully Connected, Backpropagation Neural Network," 61–68; Allen, "Transitive Inference in Animals," 175–86; Penn and Povinelli, "Causal Cognition in Human and Nonhuman Animals," 97–118; and Lind, "What Can Associative Learning Do for Planning?," 1–14.

44. For a somewhat recent explanation and review of dual-system theories, see

associative and intuitive processes. The other system, System 2, involves rule-based and analytical processes. System 1 processes are thought to be automatic and nonconscious, while System 2 processes are thought to be controlled and conscious.[45]

Dual-process and dual-system theories have been prominent in the field of psychology for decades, starting in the late 1970s.[46] Researchers argue for these theories mainly based on findings from studies performed on human reasoning processes.[47] But there are dual-system theorists who believe that System 2 processes are evolutionarily late and uniquely human.[48] For example, Jonathan Evans explains,

> It is evident that humans resemble other animals in some respects but are very different in others. Quite obviously, no other animal can engage in the forms of abstract hypothetical thought that underlie science, engineering, literature, and many other human activities. More basically, we propose that other animals are much more limited in their metarepresentational and simulation abilities, thus leading to limitations (compared with humans) in their ability to carry out forms of behavior that depend on prior appraisal of possible consequences. Thus, a key defining feature of Type 2 processing—the feature that makes humans unique—is cognitive decoupling: the ability to distinguish supposition from belief and to aid rational choices by running thought experiments.[49]

There are many critics of dual theories despite the major influence these theories have in psychology. Opponents have argued that dual theories are often formulated using vague terms, contain unreliably aligned attributes (i.e., supposed attributes of System 1 and 2 are not consistently observed together), view different processes as types when they should view them as styles, and are supported by ambiguous or unconvincing

---

Frankish, "Dual-Process and Dual-System Theories of Reasoning," 914–26.

45. Frankish, "Dual-Process and Dual-System Theories of Reasoning," 914.

46. Frankish, "Dual-Process and Dual-System Theories of Reasoning," 916; Evans and Stanovich, "Dual-Process Theories of Higher Cognition," 223.

47. See Epstein, "Integration of the Cognitive and the Psychodynamic Unconscious," 709–24; Smith and DeCoster, "Dual-Process Models in Social and Cognitive Psychology," 108–31; Kruglanski and Orehek, "Partitioning the Domain of Social Inference," 291–316; and Frankish, "Dual-Process and Dual-System Theories of Reasoning," 914–26.

48. For examples see Evans and Over, *Rationality and Reasoning*; Evans, *Thinking Twice*; and Stanovich, *Rationality and the Reflective Mind*.

49. Evans and Stanovich, "Dual-Process Theories of Higher Cognition," 236.

evidence.[50] These critics often suggest that the evidence for dual theories can be replaced with single-process theories.[51]

However, Evans and Stanovich emphasize that these critics often overgeneralize and make attacks that are aimed at all dual theories but that do not apply to many of the nuanced dual-theory positions.[52] Evans and Stanovich argue there is plenty of evidence to be found that supports a carefully defined dual-process theory. Evans and Stanovich conclude that "the evidence [for dual-process theories] is compelling and ... a very clear theoretical basis for the two-process distinction has now emerged. Such theories can account for a wide range of phenomena in the reasoning, judgment, and decision-making literatures that have been the subject of several recent books."[53]

Although the debate continues regarding whether animals are capable of abstract reasoning, there is plenty of evidence to support the conclusion that nonhuman animals most likely are not capable of such reasoning. Although it might appear that they are able to perform what could be labelled as logical reasoning, there is often an explanation for their behavior that does not necessitate invoking abstract logic. At a minimum, it is reasonable to conclude that nonhuman animals do not act rationally, and instead are guided by System 1 processes.

Self-Awareness

There are several theories regarding which attributes would provide evidence of self-awareness if found in nonhuman animals. The most widely researched include whether nonhuman animals possess mind-reading capabilities (i.e., theory of mind), mirror self-recognition, metacognition,

---

50. Evans and Stanovich, "Dual-Process Theories of Higher Cognition," 227.

51. For examples see Kruglanski et al., "Parametric Unimodel of Human Judgment," 137–61; Osman, "Evaluation of Dual-Process Theories of Reasoning," 988–1010; Keren and Schul, "Two Is Not Always Better Than One," 533–50; Kruglanski and Gigerenzer, "Intuitive and Deliberate Judgments Are Based on Common Principles," 97–109; and Carruthers, "Animal Minds Are Real," 233–48.

52. Evans and Stanovich, "Dual-Process Theories of Higher Cognition," 223–35.

53. Evans and Stanovich, "Dual-Process Theories of Higher Cognition," 237.

and episodic memory.[54] In what follows, I will mainly discuss the debates regarding nonhuman animal metacognition and episodic memory.[55]

Metacognition

An area of research that is extremely pertinent to this chapter is the scientific and philosophical study of human and nonhuman metacognition. As with rationality, there is more than one understanding of metacognition in the literature. *Metacognition* is often narrowly defined as "thinking about one's own thoughts." More broadly, Joëlle Proust defines *metacognition* as "the kinds of processes involved, and the self-knowledge gained, in thinking about, and in controlling, one's own thinking."[56]

However, it is highly debated as to what qualifies as metacognition. Some researchers believe that metacognition necessarily involves representing one's own mental states as mental states.[57] This is known as the self-attributive view. A self-attributive thought would be a self-referential second-order representation of a first-order representation (e.g., "I believe that I know/perceive/believe/feel/etc. that it is raining"[58]). Other researchers believe that metacognition merely requires controlling and monitoring one's cognitive processes.[59] This is thought to possibly involve nonconceptual, representational processes and is known as the self-evaluative view.

The main debate regarding nonhuman animals and metacognition is not whether they are capable of self-attributive metacognition, but whether they are capable of self-evaluative metacognition. Accordingly, many

---

54. For a good discussion of contemporary research into animal self-consciousness, see Andrews, *Animal Mind*, 70–77.

55. I will not discuss mirror self-recognition because I do not think it provides compelling evidence for self-awareness. Skeptical researchers have argued nonhuman animals might simply recognize their own bodies and not their own selves (Heyes, "Reflections on Self-Recognition in Primates," 915) or that their body and the body in the mirror are similar (for example see Suddendorf and Butler, "Nature of Visual Self-Recognition," 121–27). Similarly, as will be shown below, it seems that self-recognition can be explained through anoetic awareness instead of autonoetic awareness. Also, I will not discuss nonhuman animal mind-reading because metacognition and episodic memory are more pertinent to Aquinas's concepts.

56. Proust, "Metacognition," 989.

57. Proust, "Metacognition," 989.

58. Arango-Muñoz, "Two Levels of Metacognition," 73.

59. Proust, "Metacognition," 989.

researchers argue that nonhuman animals are capable of self-evaluative metacognition.[60] For example, in one study conducted by Kazuo Fujita, two tufted capuchin monkeys were tested for the ability to recognize their own memories.[61] In the study, they were presented with a sample shape on a computer screen. After a delayed period of time, they were given the choice to bring up a screen that would present them with nine shapes (one of which matched the initial shape) or bring up a screen that had an escape button. If they chose the matching task and then correctly chose the matching shape, they were rewarded with food 100 percent of the time. If they chose the wrong shape, they received nothing, and a buzzer sounded for half a second. If they chose the escape screen, they were rewarded with food 50 to 75 percent of the time. One of the monkeys was found to reliably opt out of the matching task when there was a significant enough delay between the initial shape and the choice screen. If the delay between the screens was short enough, the same monkey regularly chose the matching task and its accompanied guaranteed reward for a correct answer. This suggests that capuchins are capable of monitoring and/or recognizing their own memory traces.[62] However, Fujita noted that the capuchins seemed to only have access to the strength of their memories and not the contents. Although they seemed to possess metacognitive abilities regarding their memories, these were limited.

Other researchers believe that apparently self-evaluative behaviors in nonhuman animals are explainable through associative processes alone without metacognition.[63] For example, David Smith notes it is possible that the rewards coinciding with the escape option, in experiments like Fujita's, become more attractive as the monkeys associate them with an easier reward.[64] Also, Mike Le Pelley argues that the behavior of the monkeys can be

---

60. For examples see Shields et al., "Uncertain Responses by Humans and Rhesus Monkeys," 147–64; Hampton, "Rhesus Monkeys Know When They Remember," 5359–62; Washburn et al., "Rhesus Monkeys Immediately Generalize," 185–89; Smith et al., "Dissociating Uncertainty Responses and Reinforcement Signals," 282–97; and Kornell et al., "Transfer of Metacognitive Skill and Hint Seeking in Monkeys," 64–71.

61. Fujita, "Metamemory in Tufted Capuchin Monkeys," 575–85.

62. Fujita, "Metamemory in Tufted Capuchin Monkeys," 583–84.

63. For examples see Carruthers, "Meta-Cognition in Animals," 58–89; Hampton, "Multiple Demonstrations of Metacognition in Nonhumans," 17–28; Jozefowiez et al., "Metacognition in Animals," 29–39; Le Pelley, "Metacognitive Monkeys or Associative Animals?," 686–708.

64. Smith, "Study of Animal Metacognition," 390.

explained in that they learn to associate harder trials with unpleasant stimuli, such as the buzzer sound.[65] Thus, instead of monitoring the strength of their memories, it is possible that the monkeys are simply learning to associate longer waiting periods with unpleasant buzzer noises.

Regardless, there are many researchers who believe that nonhuman animals lack the physiological capacity for metacognition.[66] Indeed, the evidence has led some to formulate bold hypotheses in regard to human uniqueness. For example, philosopher Derek Penn, psychologist Keith Holyoak, and psychologist Daniel Povinelli have proposed what they call the relational reinterpretation hypothesis.[67] The hypothesis entails that "the discontinuity between human and nonhuman minds extends . . . to any cognitive capability that requires reinterpreting perceptual relations in terms of higher-order, structural, role-governed relations."[68] In particular the hypothesis suggests that

> animals of many taxa employ functionally compositional, particular-involving, syntactically structured mental representations about observable features, entities, and relations in the world around them. Furthermore, they form abstract representations about statistical regularities they perceive in the behavior of certain classes of physical objects (e.g., observable causal relations) and other animate agents (e.g., affiliative interactions) and are capable of using these representations off-line to make decisions in a flexible, reliable, and ecologically rational (i.e., adaptive) fashion. Human animals alone, however, possess the additional capability of reinterpreting these perceptually grounded representations in terms of higher-order, role-governed, inferentially systematic, explicitly structural relations—or, to be more precise, of approximating these higher-order features of a PSS [physical symbol system], subject to the evolved, content-specific biases and processing capacity limitations of the human brain.[69]

---

65. Le Pelley, "Metacognitive Monkeys or Associative Animals?," 686.

66. For examples see Povinelli and Vonk, "Chimpanzee Minds: Suspiciously Human?," 157–60; Povinelli and Vonk, "We Don't Need a Microscope," 385–412; Carruthers, "Meta-Cognition in Animals," 58–89; Call and Tomasello, "Does the Chimpanzee Have a Theory of Mind?," 187–92; and Bermúdez, "Mindreading in the Animal Kingdom," 145–64.

67. Penn et al., "Darwin's Mistake," 127–29.

68. Penn et al., "Darwin's Mistake," 127.

69. Penn et al., "Darwin's Mistake," 127.

In addition to the hypothesis of Penn et al., Santiago Arango-Muñoz believes the evidence supports a two-level view of metacognition that is compatible with dual-process theories.[70] He believes the self-attributive/self-evaluative debate is the result of both sides arguing that only one view is correct, when both views are correct in that each describes a distinct level of metacognition. Similar to dual-process theories, Arango-Muñoz proposes that the self-attributive view is describing a high-level (System 2) form of metacognition where subjects use concepts and theories to interpret their behavior.[71] The self-evaluative view describes the low-level (System 1) form of metacognition where feelings guide their subjects to adjust cognitive activities without engaging in second-order thought.[72] He believes that nonhuman animals are only capable of low-level metacognition, while humans are capable of both low- and high-level metacognition.

Similarly, Janet Metcalfe and Lisa Son believe the evidence suggests a distinction between anoetic, noetic, and autonoetic metacognition.[73] Anoetic metacognition involves judgments that are stimulus bound, which are spatially and temporally bound to the current time.[74] In other words, it is an animal making judgments about what it is currently experiencing. Noetic metacognition involves making judgments about representations of objects and events that are not physically present.[75] Finally, autonoetic metacognition involves self-referential judgments (similar to self-attributive metacognition). Metcalfe and Son discuss that there is insufficient evidence to conclude nonhuman animals are capable of autonoetic metacognition and that it is even debated whether nonhuman animals possess anoetic and noetic metacognitive abilities.

The existence of hypotheses such as these indicates the amount and compelling nature of the evidence against higher forms of nonhuman animal metacognition. Also, it is striking that some researchers believe the evidence points to dual types of metacognition in humans and nonhuman animals. These hypotheses and opinions add to the strength of dual-process theories regarding rationality. As it stands, nonhuman animals are not viewed as serious candidates for self-attributive or autonoetic metacognition.

70. Arango-Muñoz, "Two Levels of Metacognition," 71–82.
71. Arango-Muñoz, "Two Levels of Metacognition," 77.
72. Arango-Muñoz, "Two Levels of Metacognition," 77.
73. Metcalfe and Son, "Anoetic, Noetic, and Autonoetic Metacognition," 289–301.
74. Metcalfe and Son, "Anoetic, Noetic, and Autonoetic Metacognition," 291.
75. Metcalfe and Son, "Anoetic, Noetic, and Autonoetic Metacognition," 292.

The Nature of the Animal Soul

Episodic Memory

Besides self-attributive metacognition, episodic memory is probably one of the most promising attributes that indicates self-awareness. Episodic memory is a type of memory in which the subject remembering an event remembers the event from the subject's perspective. This is distinguished from semantic memory, which is simply remembering facts about the world apart from personal experience. Episodic memory is associated with self-awareness for reasons already mentioned; when people remember that events have happened to them, they develop a diachronic unity of consciousness over time.

Many researchers have argued there is evidence of episodic (or episodic-like) memory in nonhuman animals.[76] For example, one study involved testing for episodic memory in scrub jays, which are known for their food-caching abilities.[77] The scrub jays were allowed to cache differing types of food that were either perishable (mealworms and crickets) or nonperishable (peanuts). The study showed that if the scrub jays were released before their preferred food became inedible, they would return to the locations of their preferred food. If they were released after their preferred food became inedible, they would only return to their non-preferred food caches. These findings suggested that, at the least, the scrub jays remembered the where, what, and when aspects of their food caching.[78] This is thought to be evidence of episodic-like memory and possibly episodic memory.

However, similar to metacognition, some researchers believe it is possible to explain episodic-like behavior in simpler terms.[79] For example, it is possible the scrub jays simply possess real-time semantic (nonpersonal) knowledge of the locations and ages of their food caches.[80] Recalling the possibilities involving the capuchins and their memories, it is possible the scrub jays learned to associate longer time intervals with rotten food. Thus, they

---

76. For examples see Clayton and Dickinson, "Episodic-Like Memory During Cache Recovery by Scrub Jays," 272–74; Babb and Crystal, "Episodic-Like Memory in the Rat," 1317–21; Martin-Ordas et al., "Keeping Track of Time," 331–40; Feeney et al., "Mechanisms of What-Where-When Memory in Black-Capped Chickadees," 308–16; and Crystal et al., "Source Memory in the Rat," 387–91.

77. Clayton et al., "Elements of Episodic-Like Memory in Animals," 1483–91.

78. Clayton et al., "Elements of Episodic-Like Memory in Animals," 1490.

79. For examples, see Eichenbaum and Fortin, "Episodic Memory and the Hippocampus," 53–57; Suddendorf and Busby, "Mental Time Travel in Animals?," 391–96; and Hampton and Schwartz, "Episodic Memory in Nonhumans," 192–97.

80. Hampton and Schwartz, "Episodic Memory in Nonhumans," 194.

could simply return to food caches of which they possess stronger memories or perishable food caches only when shorter intervals have lapsed.[81]

One of the most interesting aspects of episodic memory, and also relevant to this chapter, is that episodic memory has been found to coincide with the ability to mentally time-travel. Mental time-travel is the ability to remember or to imagine oneself in the past or the future. Psychologists believe that the two coincide due in part to studies involving damage to the human brain.

For example, in 1981, a man known as K. C. was involved in a motorcycle accident in which he suffered brain damage.[82] K. C. exhibits a rare type of retrograde amnesia in which he cannot remember anything that has happened to him from a personal perspective (episodic memory), although he retains knowledge of facts about the world and himself (semantic memory). For example, K. C. knows the address and appearance of the house in which he spent his first nine years of life, but he does not remember a single event that took place there. Moreover, K. C. has a similar problem regarding thinking about his future. Endel Tulving explains,

> K.C. cannot think about his own personal future. Thus, when asked, he cannot tell the questioner what he is going to do later on that day, or the day after, or at any time in the rest of his life, any more than he can say what he did the day before or what events have happened in his life. When he is asked to describe the state of his mind when he thinks about his future, whether the next 15 minutes or the next year, he again says that it is "blank."[83]

Studies of K. C. have led researchers to conclude that episodic and semantic memory are based in different sets of neural mechanisms.[84] Thus, if humans or nonhuman animals possess semantic memory, this does not necessarily entail that they will possess episodic memory. Also, as mentioned, K. C.'s case has led to the conclusion that episodic memory is necessary for mental time-travel. This is striking because it entails that if nonhuman animals do not possess the ability for episodic memory, then they not only cannot remember the past from a personal perspective, but they also cannot think of or anticipate future personal events. As will be

---

81. Eichenbaum and Fortin, "Episodic Memory and the Hippocampus," 55.
82. See Rosenbaum et al., "Case of K.C.," 989–1021.
83. Tulving, "Episodic Memory and Autonoesis," 26.
84. Tulving, "Episodic Memory and Autonoesis," 24.

explained below, this has major implications for the problem of animal suffering and the status of nonhuman animals regarding moral agency.

Additionally, Tulving emphasizes that the capacity for episodic memory does not just enable personal mental time travel, but also enables a present sense of self. He notes,

> To describe autonoetic consciousness with regards to episodic memory, there is a natural bias to cast the discussion in terms of awareness of the past. Autonoetic consciousness is not limited to the past, however; it encompasses the capacity to represent the self's experiences in the past, present, and future. When one is autonoetically aware of one's experiences in the past, one recollects the past and, therefore, retrieves information from episodic memory. But also dependent on autonoetic consciousness and, we argue, closely related to episodic memory is the ability to be aware of the self's present.[85]

Thus, the absence of episodic memory in nonhuman animals not only suggests that they are not able to personally experience the past and future, but also unable to personally experience the present.

Similar to rationality and metacognition, some researchers believe that episodic memory and the ability for personal mental time-travel are unique to humans.[86] This is another area where the evidence points to dual-processes in humans and nonhuman animals. Regarding memory, it seems that some nonhuman animals have episodic-like memory (knowing the impersonal where, what, and when of events), while humans uniquely possess both episodic-like and episodic memory. For example, Tulving explains,

> Many kinds of complex behaviors of many kinds of animals can be, and have been, interpreted as manifesting episodic memory, and in many cases these behaviors do have many features in common with behaviors that are grounded in episodic memory. Practically invariably, however, the same behaviors can also be interpreted more parsimoniously, as manifestations of semantic or declarative memory, which do not provide for, and do not require postulation of, the apprehension of subjective past or subjective future time.[87]

---

85. Wheeler et al., "Toward a Theory of Episodic Memory," 335.

86. For examples see Roberts, "Are Animals Stuck in Time?," 473–89; Suddendorf and Busby, "Mental Time Travel in Animals?," 391–96; Tulving, "Episodic Memory and Autonoesis," 3–56; Suddendorf and Corballis, "Evolution of Foresight," 299–313.

87. Tulving, "Episodic Memory and Autonoesis," 48.

Thus, to date, it seems that most, if not all, nonhuman animals do not have the capability for self-awareness that is found in humans. For one, the evidence suggests that humans uniquely possess the ability for higher-order metacognition. Nonhuman animals are not able to think about their thoughts and are, thus, unaware of themselves as the possessors of such thoughts. Additionally, episodic memory is believed to be unique to humans. This entails that nonhuman animals cannot remember the past as it happened to them personally or personally experience the present. This also means nonhuman animals are unable to anticipate or think about their personal futures.

Implications of Neo-Thomism for the Problem of Animal Suffering

So, the Thomistic view of nonhuman animals needs updating. It certainly is outdated to explain animal cognition and behavior solely through the broad term *estimative power*. However, the crucial aspects of the Thomistic view of nonhuman animals are in no danger of replacement.

In light of the Thomistic view of nonhuman animal minds, there is no evidence that proves nonhuman animals possess either higher-order (System 2) rationality or higher-order abilities associated with self-awareness, such as self-attributive or autonoetic metacognition and episodic memory. Thus, nonhuman animals are neither rational, nor have higher-order access to their mental states, nor can remember or imagine themselves in the past, present, or future. This is similar to the neo-Cartesian option (3): "Some nonhuman creatures have states that have intrinsic phenomenal qualities analogous to those possessed by humans when they are in states of pain. These creatures lack, however, any higher-order states of being aware of themselves as being in first-order states."

Thus, the evidence suggests that there is no problem of animal suffering; Rowe's premise (1) is false. If nonhuman animals are neither rational nor self-aware, then they are not suffering as persons. For one, nonhuman animals lack higher-order access to their suffering regardless of whether it is experienced phenomenally or not. If nonhuman animals are incapable of higher-order thoughts regarding their lower-order experiences, this means that nonhuman animals are incapable of higher-order thoughts, such as, "I believe that I feel pain," or, "I believe that I wish to avoid pain." As humans, we have higher-order access to our lower-order mental states throughout

The Nature of the Animal Soul

our lives. So, it is hard to imagine what this would be like. However, the nonhuman animal lack of self-attributive or autonoetic metacognition sheds light on the nonpersonal nature of nonhuman animal experiences. As Aquinas argues, nonhuman animals do not know that they know or make judgments in a self-referential manner. As hard as it is to imagine, there are experiences of pain and suffering in nonhuman animals, but there are no personal thoughts/experiences/awarenesses of these experiences.

Also, nonhuman animals are incapable of abstract rationality. This is relevant to the problem of animal suffering in that nonlinguistic creatures could never form abstract concepts regarding their suffering. For instance, arational animals cannot reach the understanding that they ought not to be in a state of pain or suffering. Moreover, it is important to remember that their lack of rationality entails that they do not act for logical reasons. Thus, arational animals cannot be said to have any logical reasons for acting in ways that avoid future experiences of pain. Pain behaviors are simply explainable through associative learning and, at most, anoetic and noetic metacognition.

In addition to the Thomistic distinctives of metacognition and rationality, it was found that nonhuman animals lack episodic memory and, thus, any sense of a personal past, present, and future. If they experience pain and suffering, this is only experienced in a nonpersonal present. Nonhuman animals neither self-referentially remember suffering they have experienced, nor self-referentially experience current suffering, nor self-referentially anticipate future suffering they may encounter. This is evidence for Aquinas's notion that nonhuman animals lack a sense of self, diachronic or otherwise, because they are not aware of a personal process of abstracting and storing knowledge of universals.[88]

These considerations not only provide an answer to the problem of animal suffering as it relates to nonhuman animal pain, but also as it relates to any other type of suffering that nonhuman animals might experience, such as fear, sorrow, and others. If nonhuman animals are not self-aware, then they lack higher-order access to any of these unpleasant states. Thus, Rowe's premise (1) is false; there is no person, *qua* person, who experiences pain or suffering in the nonhuman animal kingdom; and nonhuman

---

88. For further evidence along these lines see Markowitsch and Staniloiu, "Memory, Autonoetic Consciousness, and the Self," 16–39. Markowitsch and Staniloiu argue that autonoetic consciousness and episodic memory are required for episodic-autobiographical memory (EAM) (i.e., a diachronic sense of self) and that EAM is probably unique to humans.

animal suffering is morally insignificant, so God has no moral obligation to prevent it.

An Objection to the Neo-Thomistic Solution

A major objection at this point could be that the neo-Thomistic concept of arational and nonpersonal animals does not avoid the problem. For example, when arguing against neo-Cartesian option (3) (which it was noted is similar to the neo-Thomistic position), Robert Francescotti says,

> it is not clear that position 3 is even coherent. We are to imagine that some other animals have mental states with "intrinsic phenomenal qualities analogous to those possessed by humans," but they are not aware of being in those states, and so, Murray explains, "there is simply no victim or subject for whom it can be said that there is a way it is like for it to be in such a state of pain" (Murray 2008, 56). However, if these states are phenomenally similar to those we have, as 3 claims, then there would be a "what it is like" character to these states, and in particular they would have something similar to the distressful feel of our pain states. So there would be a clear sense in which some other animals suffer.[89]

Regardless of whether nonhuman animals are persons, if they are experiencing unpleasant mental and physical states, then the evils remain. This objection, however, seems to be avoidable through noting important distinctions and reemphasizing the Thomistic concept of consciousness.

First, it will be helpful to discuss a distinction that has been emphasized by Endel Tulving. Tulving and his associates make a careful distinction between consciousness and awareness. He says that consciousness is "a general capacity that an individual possesses for particular kinds of mental representations and subjective experiences."[90] Awareness is "a particular manifestation or expression of this general capacity."[91] Tulving et al. explain,

> Consciousness, like other capacities of living systems, has no object; it is not directed at anything. It is like a stage that allows some actions, but not others, to take place on it, but it does not prescribe action. Awareness always has an object; it is always of something. Thus, awareness presumes consciousness, but consciousness does

---

89. Francescotti, "Problem of Animal Pain and Suffering," 115–16.
90. Wheeler et al., "Toward a Theory of Episodic Memory," 335.
91. Wheeler et al., "Toward a Theory of Episodic Memory," 335.

not imply awareness: Consciousness is a necessary but not sufficient condition of awareness.[92]

Accordingly, I have been careful throughout this chapter to use the terms *consciousness* and *self-awareness* when referring to humans and nonhuman animals.

Regardless, Francescotti says that pain states having a "what it is like" character are "clear" cases of nonhuman animal suffering. But it is not clear that these are "clear" cases of suffering. This is because, as concluded above, it is likely that nonhuman animals are *conscious* of pain, but not self-referentially *aware* of their pain. If nonhuman animals lack metacognitive abilities, then they can only be conscious of pain and suffering. Pain and suffering would be just one part of the kaleidoscope of their conscious experience. They would react to it according to their instincts and associatively learned behavior. If they possess lower-order metacognitive abilities, then they can be aware, yet not self-referentially aware, of pain and suffering. They would experience, focus upon, and make judgments regarding pain and suffering, yet they would not do this on a personal level.

Tulving's three levels of consciousness and awareness are helpful here as well (i.e., anoetic, noetic, and autonoetic). He explains that anoetic consciousness "is temporally and spatially bound to the current situation. Organisms possessing only anoetic consciousness are conscious in the sense that they are capable of perceptually registering, internally representing, and behaviourally responding to aspects of the present environment, both external and internal."[93] Also, "Noetic consciousness allows an organism to be aware of, and to cognitively operate on, objects and events, and relations among objects and events, in the absence of these objects and events. The organism can flexibly act upon such symbolic knowledge of the world." As explained, nonhuman animals possess anoetic consciousness and possibly noetic consciousness, but not autonoetic consciousness.

If neo-Cartesian option (3) is necessarily tied to the "intrinsic phenomenal qualities" of states possessed by nonhuman animals, then perhaps Francescotti's objection holds here. But as explained above, a neo-Thomistic understanding of nonhuman animals does not necessarily focus on "what it is like" for nonhuman animals to experience the world, but only that they are conscious. Thus, regardless of whether autonoetic consciousness is the only type of consciousness accompanied with qualia, noetic or

92. Wheeler et al., "Toward a Theory of Episodic Memory," 335.
93. Tulving, "Memory and Consciousness," 3.

anoetic consciousness is all that is needed to meet the Thomistic standard for consciousness.

However, even if there is "something it is like" for animals to experience pain and suffering, this does not mean that the experience is necessarily intrinsically evil. Getting back to Francescotti's objection, as mentioned, it is not clear that the anoetic and noetic experience of pain and suffering constitutes suffering. This can be shown by emphasizing two Thomistic concepts.

Evil as Privation

The first concept is the evil-as-privation view covered in chapter 2. As discussed, Aquinas defines *evil* as "the absence of the good, which is natural and due to a thing,"[94] and emphasizes that not all absences of good are evil, although all evils are absences of some good. It was shown in chapter 2 that nonhuman animal pain and suffering is incorrectly assumed to be evil by proponents of the problem of animal suffering. But the sensation of pain is thought to be a homeostatic emotion, similar to itching, hunger, and thirst.[95] Without pain, the lifespan of most nonhuman animals would be significantly shorter.[96] Additionally, researchers believe that other types of suffering, such as sadness, fear, and even depression, are likewise homeostatic emotional responses that are conducive to physical and social survival.[97] Nonhuman animal pain and suffering helps nonhuman animals to flourish, and even seemingly maladaptive instances of pain and suffering have been found to give their subjects survival advantages.

It is easy to conclude that God, as the creator of all human and nonhuman life, intended for animals to possess the abilities to anoetically and noetically experience pain and suffering. He endowed his creatures with these homeostatic emotions so they would flourish in their natural environments.[98] In this way, pain and other forms of suffering are not evil, since

---

94. *ST* I, q. 49, a. 1.

95. Craig, "New View of Pain as a Homeostatic Emotion," 303–7.

96. For example, see Nagasako et al., "Congenital Insensitivity to Pain," 213–19.

97. For examples, see Schwarz, "Warmer and More Social," 245; Keltner and Kring, "Emotion, Social Function, and Psychopathology," 324; Öhman and Mineka, "Fears, Phobias, and Preparedness," 483; and Allen and Badcock, "Darwinian Models of Depression," 819.

98. To be clear, I am not saying that pain and suffering are good in the sense that they ought to be sought for their own sakes. Instead, they are instrumental goods that help creatures flourish.

God wills creatures to possess these metaphysically and instrumentally good abilities. Both humans and nonhuman animals experience pain and suffering, although nonhuman animals do not self-referentially experience pain and suffering.

Suffering as the Privation of the Willed Good

The second concept involves free will. There is a particular sense in which Aquinas thought pain and suffering could be viewed as evils. For example, in the *ST*, Aquinas mentions that evils are rightly divided into two categories: evils of punishment and evils of fault. In describing evils of punishment, Aquinas says,

> intellectual creatures also suffer evil when they are deprived of forms or dispositions or anything else potentially necessary for good activity, whether the things belong to the soul or the body or external things. And such evil, in the judgment of the Catholic faith, needs to be called punishment.
> For three things belong to the nature of a punishment.... The second characteristic of the nature of punishment is that it is contrary to the will of the one suffering punishment. For everyone's will inclines to seek the person's own good, and so it is contrary to one's will to be deprived of one's own good.[99]

Here Aquinas is explaining that natural evils are rightly called punishments in humans because the deprivation of the form or disposition of a human is against the will. In other words, no human wants to experience natural evils in his own body. This would include the experience of pain and suffering because such things are unwanted, unpleasant, and entail a loss of user-control.

However, if nonhuman animals do not possess immaterial intellects, and all their actions are determined by the laws of nature, then they cannot possess free will. Pain and suffering cannot be evils for them, in the subjective sense, because they can neither understand that they are in pain nor freely will to stop experiencing it. Of course, it may appear that they will to avoid pain as humans do, but they are not willing in a morally relevant sense because their pain-avoidance behavior is due to lower-order processes and not the higher-order wish to avoid the lower-order suffering.

---

99. *De Malo*, q. 1, a. 4.

Thus, from a Thomistic perspective, nonhuman animal pain and suffering are not evil. They are not intrinsically evil states because they are metaphysically good physiological processes that are natural to nonhuman animals and necessary for flourishing. Also, they are not evil in that they are not experienced self-referentially by nonhuman animals and cannot be against the will of nonhuman animals because nonhuman animals do not possess free will.

Before concluding, it will be good to note an interesting aspect of this neo-Thomistic answer to the problem of animal suffering. As the evidence suggests, it is most likely that nonhuman animals are neither rational nor self-aware. While there are a few promising candidates, such as dolphins, elephants, and great apes, the majority of nonhuman animals are not considered to be possibly self-conscious.

Yet if it were conclusively determined that one of these candidates were in fact self-aware, it would not overturn this neo-Thomistic answer to the problem of animal suffering. This is because if it were determined that a nonhuman animal is rational and self-aware, this would entail that the nonhuman animal would possess a rational soul along with an immaterial intellect. The reason why it would not be problematic is because Aquinas believed that rational animals can survive the death of their bodies due to the immateriality of the intellect.[100]

Thus, if a nonhuman animal were found to be rational and self-aware, it would follow that such an animal could participate in the resurrection of the dead at the end of days. Indeed, if a nonhuman animal is found to be rational, it ceases to be a nonhuman animal and should be classified as a human in the sense that it would be a rational animal. Traditional theodicies concerning humans and how they relate to natural and moral evil would apply to such an animal.

Since rational, nonlinguistic animals would possess IQs much lower than *homo sapiens* (meaning they are morally inculpable), and since nonlinguistic animals could never understand the gospel message, it follows from God's justice that they would live in the new heavens and new earth with human saints at the end of days. Their rational souls would make it possible to survive the death of their physical bodies, and their moral inculpability would ensure they could not be punished for wrongdoings. Thus, a relatively short life involving suffering would ultimately result in eternal life in the presence of God. The suffering of rational non-*homo-sapiens* animals

---

100. *ST* I, q. 75, a. 6; *SCG* II, c. 79–81; *De anima*, a. 14.

(if such creatures were found to exist) would be allowed by God for the purpose of communicating his goodness. Perhaps God decided that the hierarchy of beings he creates to achieve his purpose should include rational nonhuman animals.[101] So even if a theist is in doubt as to the personhood of any particular nonhuman animal, he can conclude that if the non-*homo-sapiens* animal is self-aware, the animal will ultimately experience a fate similar to humans who join God in eternity.

Conclusion

Chapter 2 revealed that nonhuman animal pain and suffering is not evil. Pain and suffering are metaphysically good and have been found to help nonhuman animals to flourish in a world governed by physical laws. Yet, this left the question as to whether an infinitely powerful and loving God would allow nonhuman animal suffering due to its unpleasantness.

In this chapter, it was shown that the philosophy of Thomas Aquinas, along with contemporary philosophical and scientific evidence, provides an answer to this question. Aquinas believed that the difference between human and nonhuman animals lies in that the former possess rational souls, and the latter merely possess sensitive souls. As rational animals, humans possess immaterial intellects, which endow them with the abilities of rationality and self-awareness. The lack of an immaterial intellect makes it so that nonhuman animals are neither rational nor self-aware and, therefore, lack moral agency and personhood.

Contemporary philosophical and scientific evidence supports Aquinas's medieval theory of nonhuman animal minds. The evidence suggests that nonhuman animals are incapable of abstract reasoning and lack higher-order metacognitive abilities and episodic memory. As such, nonhuman animals do not experience pain and suffering as persons. They do not have higher-order access to their lower-order mental states, and they cannot self-referentially remember or anticipate painful experiences. Also, they cannot come to the understanding that they ought not to be in pain.

It could be objected that this does not solve the problem since animals are phenomenologically aware of pain and suffering. However, it was shown that this cannot be understood as evil because pain and suffering are

---

101. The Thomistic concepts of God's purpose for the universe, the necessity of a hierarchy of beings, what it means for God to "communicate his goodness," and what these entail for the problem of animal suffering will be discussed in chapter 4.

metaphysically and instrumentally good physiological processes. Pain and suffering are not evil because they are not privations of proper goods and are conducive to flourishing. Moreover, pain and other unpleasant states are not evils in nonhuman animals because nonhuman animals do not possess free will.

The evidence suggests that nonhuman animals are most likely not self-aware, and there is no problem of animal suffering; Rowe's premise (1) is false because there are no instances of intense suffering that an all-powerful and wholly good God should prevent. However, even if a certain kind of nonhuman animal were found to possess self-awareness, this would not eliminate the neo-Thomistic answer. Instead, all it would entail is that the certain kind of animal would most likely be rewarded with eternal life at the end of days. Thus, not only does a neo-Thomistic view of nonhuman animals provide an answer to the problem of animal suffering, but it also provides a more compelling answer in contrast to neo-Cartesianism. Most researchers believe that nonhuman animals are conscious, but few, if any, believe that nonhuman animals are self-aware like humans.

As mentioned at the end of chapter 2, a question might remain as to why God would make a world with contingent creatures that are susceptible to suffering and death in which it is necessary to make design tradeoffs. The next chapter will attempt to answer this question. It will also cover Paul Draper's inference-to-the-best-explanation argument from nonhuman animal suffering.

4

Animal Suffering and God's Purpose for the Universe[1]

IN PREVIOUS CHAPTERS, IT was shown that there is no way to know if God is obligated to prevent intense nonhuman animal pain and suffering; nonhuman animal pain and suffering is not evil because it increases nonhuman animal flourishing; and, even though pain and suffering is unpleasant, nonhuman animals are not aware of themselves as subjects that experience pain and suffering. The problem of animal suffering as formulated by William Rowe is not problematic for classical theism. Yet it has not been explained why the world is the way it is. Why did an all-loving, all-powerful, and all-knowing God create a world governed by physical laws containing mortal creatures that experience pain and suffering?

As explained in chapter 1, there are several strategies that theists have used to answer the problem of animal suffering, including the neo-Cartesian denial of nonhuman animal suffering and arguments for the necessity of nomic regularity. However, most strategies merely provide an explanation for the existence of nonhuman animal suffering. Few theists have tried to counter arguments, such as Paul Draper's, that the evidence points more toward a naturalistic world than a theistic world.[2]

This is important because even if a satisfactory explanation for the existence of nonhuman animal suffering is provided, the question of whether

---

1. Almost in its entirety, this chapter was taken from Keltz, "God's Purpose for the Universe and the Problem of Animal Suffering," 475–92.

2. The concept of nomic regularity is an example of an attempt to predict the kind of universe that a theistic God would create. But no contemporary philosophers have made arguments that are similar to Aquinas's arguments for a hierarchy of beings.

the evidence is better explained by theism or naturalism remains. Although he did not have the problem of animal suffering in mind, Thomas Aquinas proposed an explanation for the diversity and corruptibility of nature in several places in his writings. His arguments involve God's reason for creating and God's willing the perfection of the universe. Aquinas's conclusions contradict the claim that naturalism is the best explanation for the natural history of the earth.

In this chapter, I will analyze several arguments in this regard from Aquinas's writings. First, I will discuss the claim that naturalism is the preferred position given animal suffering. Next, I will introduce several preliminary concepts needed to understand Aquinas's arguments. After this, I will explain Aquinas's arguments and defend them against a major objection. Finally, I will discuss the implications the arguments have for the claim that nonhuman animal suffering points to the superiority of naturalism.

Arguments for Naturalism from Animal Suffering

As discussed in chapter 1, Paul Draper has defended several types of arguments for naturalism from nonhuman animal suffering.[3] His various arguments are formulated as evidential arguments from evil. They usually emphasize the nature of pain and pleasure and the truth of evolutionary theory to build a case for naturalism against theism.

As mentioned, in "Darwin's Argument from Evil," Draper says the theory of natural selection

> can serve as a good 'atheodicy': an explanation of various facts about good and evil that works much better on the assumption that an alternative to theism—in this case the no-design hypothesis—is true than on the assumption that orthodox theism is true.[4]

Again, Draper states that "Darwinian explanations of good and evil are less complete when Darwin's theory is combined with theism than when it is combined with the no-design hypothesis."[5] Here he is arguing that the truth of evolutionary theory provides evidence for naturalism rather than theism

---

3. See Draper, "Pain and Pleasure," 331–50; Draper, "Cosmic Fine-Tuning and Terrestrial Suffering," 311–21; Draper, "Darwin's Argument from Evil," 49–70; Draper, "Christian Theism and Life on Earth," 306–16; and Draper, "Evolution and the Problem of Evil," 271–82.

4. Draper, "Darwin's Argument from Evil," 58.

5. Draper, "Darwin's Argument from Evil," 63.

Animal Suffering and God's Purpose for the Universe

because "Darwin's theory comes closer to solving the puzzle of good and evil faced by the proponent of the no-design hypothesis than the puzzle of good and evil faced by the theist."[6]

In "Christian Theism and Life on Earth," Draper argues that the specific amount of "flourishing and floundering" of sentient organisms on earth provides evidence for naturalism over theism. He emphasizes,

> What we find when we examine our biosphere is that, for a variety of biological and ecological reasons, organisms compete for survival, with some having an advantage in the struggle for survival over others; as a result, many organisms, including many sentient beings, never flourish because they die before maturity, many others barely survive, but languish for most or all of their lives, and those that reach maturity and flourish for much of their lives usually flounder in old age; further, in the case of human beings and very probably some non-human animals as well, floundering or languishing often involves intense and prolonged suffering.[7]

Draper concludes that "the fact that huge numbers of human and other sentient beings never flourish at all before death and countless others flourish only briefly, is extremely surprising given CT [Christian theism]. It is not what one would expect to find in a living world created by the Christian God."[8]

These are good examples of arguments that emphasize the earth's natural history and conclude that naturalism is the preferred explanation for such a vast amount of nonhuman animal suffering. They are mainly concerned with the explanatory power of naturalism and theism and assume that, all else being equal, animal suffering points to theism being most likely false. So, the basic argument for naturalism from nonhuman animal suffering can be formulated as

(1) Either theism or naturalism is true.

(2) The God of theism would more than likely create a world in which sentient creatures always flourish.

(3) However, sentient creatures have suffered and died for millions of years on the earth.

(4) Therefore, naturalism is more likely than not to be true.

   6. Draper, "Darwin's Argument from Evil," 65.
   7. Draper, "Christian Theism and Life on Earth," 312.
   8. Draper, "Christian Theism and Life on Earth," 313.

As mentioned earlier, some theists have attempted to provide reasons for the existence of nonhuman animal suffering, but few have attempted to show that theism anticipates a world that contains nonhuman animal suffering. Although there are arguably plenty of philosophical, scientific, and historical reasons to accept theism (and Christian theism in particular), the argument for naturalism from animal suffering seems to stand. However, as mentioned above, the philosophy of Thomas Aquinas can provide an answer to this problem.

Preliminaries to Aquinas's Arguments

In several places in Aquinas's writings, he argues that in order to accomplish God's purpose for the universe, God must create a hierarchy of beings with differing grades of perfection.[9] At *ST* I, q. 47, a. 1, Aquinas summarizes this argument when he says,

> Hence we must say that the distinction and multitude of things come from the intention of the first agent, who is God. For He brought things into being in order that His goodness might be communicated to creatures, and be represented by them; and because His goodness could not be adequately represented by one creature alone, He produced many and diverse creatures, that what was wanting to one in the representation of the divine goodness might be supplied by another. For goodness, which in God is simple and uniform, in creatures is manifold and divided and hence the whole universe together participates the divine goodness more perfectly, and represents it better than any single creature whatever.[10]

Aquinas is arguing that for God to best communicate his goodness, God must create "many and diverse creatures." Aquinas believes this is something God must necessarily do (given God's free choice to create) to accomplish his purpose for the universe. If God did not do this, his creation would not be perfect, which is impossible because God is perfect.

Of course, this argument is more detailed than Aquinas's summary, and Aquinas has several arguments to this regard. So, it will be necessary to examine several arguments in detail. However, before this, it is necessary to discuss several concepts that Aquinas presupposes in the arguments.

9. Aquinas presents these in detail at *SCG* II, c. 45; and *ST* I, q. 47.
10. *ST* I, q. 47, a. 1.

Those who are unfamiliar with Aquinas will probably find several aspects of his summary puzzling. Aquinas mentions that God wants to communicate God's goodness, and to accomplish this God must create diverse creatures. There are three main concepts that need explaining here: the first is what Aquinas means by God's goodness; the second is God's reason for creating and purpose for the universe; and the third is the metaphysical hurdle that God encounters while accomplishing this purpose.

God's Goodness

First, Aquinas believes that God is infinite goodness. As mentioned in chapter 2, this is because of the metaphysical implications resulting from Aquinas's Five Ways. Recall that Aquinas holds to the doctrine that goodness and existence are identical. In the first part of the *ST*, Aquinas argues,

> Goodness and being are really the same, and differ only in idea; which is clear from the following argument. The essence of goodness consists in this, that it is in some way desirable. Hence the Philosopher says (Ethic. i): Goodness is what all desire. Now it is clear that a thing is desirable only in so far as it is perfect; for all desire their own perfection. But everything is perfect so far as it is actual. Therefore it is clear that a thing is perfect so far as it exists; for it is existence that makes all things actual, as is clear from the foregoing (Q. 3, A. 4; Q. 4, A. 1). Hence it is clear that goodness and being are the same really.[11]

Here Aquinas is arguing that something is only good as far as it is a desirable example of what it is supposed to be. The term *good* is an attributive adjective (as opposed to a predicative adjective) in that its meaning changes according to the noun it is intended to modify.[12] So for example, the term *good* in the phrases *good human* and *good dog* mean different but similar things. Not only are the physical attributes of a good human and a good dog different, but also humans are held to a moral standard that dogs are not.

But if something does not exist in any way, then it cannot be desirable in any way. This is why Aquinas says, "something is perfect so far as it is actual." A nonexistent thing is not desirable in any way if it neither actually exists nor potentially exists. Thus, implied in the perfection of anything

---

11. *ST* I, q. 5, a. 1.
12. Geach, "Good and Evil," 33.

is actuality, or existence, and this entails that existence and goodness are interchangeable concepts.

Aquinas's cosmological arguments conclude that there must exist a being that is not limited in any way. For example, in Aquinas's First Way, he reasons there must ultimately be something without potentiality to explain the *per se* ordered series of the actualization of potencies in the world.[13] But something without potentiality would be pure actuality. As explained above, something is good insofar as it is actual, and this entails that God is infinite goodness.

Also, in Aquinas's Second Way, he reasons there must be something without an efficient cause (i.e., something that depends on nothing else for its existence) to explain the *per se* ordered series of efficient causality in the world that causes contingent things to exist.[14] But because all contingent things have an essence that is conjoined with existence through efficient causality, something without an efficient cause can only be something in which its essence is existence. The ultimate efficient cause of the existence of all contingent things must be existence itself, or pure existence, which Aquinas took to be God. As explained above, because existence and goodness are interchangeable, if God is pure existence, then God is also infinite goodness. This is foremost a metaphysical goodness and not necessarily a moral goodness that most modern readers would think of when hearing that God is infinite goodness.

God's Reason for Creating and Purpose for Creation

Infinite metaphysical goodness is the goodness that Aquinas is referring to when he says that God aims to communicate God's goodness. But it might remain puzzling to some why Aquinas is saying that God wants "to communicate His goodness." The explanation is that Aquinas believes this is the only reason for why God would have decided to create.

One of Aquinas's reasons for believing this is his understanding that God is perfect. Because God is without potentiality and is pure actuality (i.e., infinite perfection), lacks nothing, and is complete in himself, there is nothing that God could ever need. This means that if God were to choose to create, there can be no cause for his choice to create. There can be no cause, but there can be a reason for why God wills to create.

13. *ST* I, q. 2, a. 3.
14. *ST* I, q. 2, a. 3.

Animal Suffering and God's Purpose for the Universe

But why would an infinitely perfect Being ever choose to create anything? The answer lies in the Dionysian principle that goodness is inclined to communicate itself: "But it belongs to the essence of goodness to communicate itself to others, as is plain from Dionysius (*Div. Nom.* iv). Hence it belongs to the essence of the highest good to communicate itself in the highest manner to the creature."[15] Reginald Garrigou-Lagrange provides an illustration as to why Aquinas might have agreed with this principle:

> Goodness is essentially communicative; good is diffusive of itself. In the material order, we observe that, the sun imparts its light and vivifying heat to all that comes in contact with it. In the intellectual order, when the intellect has arrived at the knowledge of truth, it spontaneously seeks to impart this to others. In the moral order, those with a holy ardor for goodness, like the Apostles, have no rest until these same aspirations, this same love, are aroused in others.[16]

Reasoning from effect to cause, Aquinas concludes that because goodness is naturally diffusive of itself, God must also be naturally inclined to create given God's infinite goodness. Thus, the reason for why God creates is that he freely wills (because he is naturally inclined) to communicate his goodness. This entails that the purpose of the universe and the entire created order is the communication of God's infinite goodness.

A Metaphysical Obstacle to Communicating Infinite Goodness

Although Aquinas believes that God is omnipotent, Aquinas does not believe it is possible for God to communicate God's goodness in certain ways. For example, Aquinas argues that although God is perfect, God cannot create an infinitely perfect world.[17] The reason for this is because, as pure actuality, only God is infinitely perfect. Anything besides God will be contingent and fall infinitely short of his perfection. In this regard, Aquinas argues that for any world we can imagine, we could just as easily imagine a world with one or two more good things.[18] Thus, there is an infinite number

---

15. *ST* III, q. 1, a. 1.
16. Garrigou-Lagrange, *God, His Existence and His Nature*, 99.
17. *SCG* II, c. 25.
18. *ST* I, q. 25, a. 6, ad3.

of worlds that God could possibly create that would each fall infinitely short of his perfection.[19]

But Aquinas does not think this means there is nothing perfect about what God creates. Although God cannot create an infinitely perfect world, Aquinas believes that God can create a perfectly ordered world. The mere existence of the world is not enough to communicate God's goodness, so God must order the world for it to fulfill his purpose. Aquinas explains,

> as *it belongs to the best to produce the best*, it is not fitting that the supreme goodness of God should produce things without giving them their perfection. Now a thing's ultimate perfection consists in the attainment of its end. Therefore it belongs to the Divine goodness, as it brought things into existence, so to lead them to their end: and this is to govern. . . . For since the end of the government of the world is that which is essentially good, which is the greatest good; the government of the world must be the best kind of government.[20]

Thus, the perfection of the universe lies in God's perfect ordering of its parts to the whole with God as its end. Aquinas believes that to do this, God must create a world with a natural law (i.e., physical laws to govern inanimate objects, plants, and animals) and a moral law (to govern humans, which have free will).[21] All of these considerations help to explain why Aquinas says that God wants to communicate God's goodness, and to accomplish this God must create diverse creatures.

Aquinas's Arguments at SCG II, c. 45

Noting the Thomistic concepts of God's goodness and purpose for creating greatly helps the transition to discussing Aquinas's arguments for the necessity of a hierarchy of beings. In Aquinas's earlier work, the *Summa contra Gentiles*, he provides several arguments to this regard. At *SCG* II, c. 45 in particular, he proposes seven arguments concluding that God must create a hierarchy of beings to accomplish God's purpose for creating.

---

19. Aquinas agrees with Aristotle and believes that an actual infinite multitude is impossible (*ST* I, q. 7, a. 4). Thus, Aquinas believes that God cannot create a universe with an actually infinite number of beings. If this possibility is eliminated, God must choose between the infinite number of universes that do not include actually infinite multitudes.

20. *ST* I, q. 103, a. 1; *ST* I, q. 103, a. 3.

21. *SCG* III, c. 114–15.

First, Aquinas argues,

> created things cannot come by a perfect likeness to God with respect to only one species of the creature, for, since the cause surpasses its effect, that which is simply and unitedly in the cause is found in the effect to have a composite and multiple nature—unless the effect reach to the species of the cause, which does not apply to the case in point, since the creature cannot be equal to God. Therefore, there was need for multiplicity and variety in things created, in order that we might find in them a perfect likeness to God according to their mode.[22]

As mentioned above, God is faced with a metaphysical hurdle with his intention to imbue his likeness into creation. God is perfect, simple, and immaterial, while his creation is imperfect, contingent, and mostly material. It does not make sense for God to make one kind of creature to accomplish this. One type or two types of creatures would do a poor job of representing his goodness. As Norman Kretzmann suggests, God's goal in creating is the equivalent of trying to "represent a geometer's straight line (which is continuous, infinite, and invisible) by nothing but pencilled dots."[23] One or two dots would not serve very well to represent the invisible line. God must create a diverse number of species because contingent creatures can only possess so many perfections. None can contain all perfections as is the case with God. Instead it follows that God would make a large variety of creatures to better demonstrate his goodness.

Next, Aquinas argues,

> Just as things made of matter are in the passive potency of matter, so things made by an agent must be in the active potency of the agent. Now the passive potency of matter would not be perfectly reduced to act if only one of those things to which matter is in potency were reduced to act. Therefore, if an agent, whose potency embraces several effects, were to make only one of them, its potency would not be so perfectly reduced to act as when it makes several. Now, the effect receives the likeness of the agent by the active potency being reduced to act. Therefore, there would not be a perfect likeness of God in the universe if all things were of one degree.[24]

---

22. *SCG* II, c. 45; cf. *ST* I, q. 47, a. 1.
23. Kretzmann, *Metaphysics of Creation*, 217.
24. *SCG* II, c. 45.

This argument is similar to his first but emphasizes all of the potencies contained within matter. Matter has the potentiality to receive any number of forms, and it would be contrary to God's purpose if he only actualized one of these forms. God is unlimited actuality, so if he wants to imbue his likeness into creation, this will entail actualizing a great variety and number of forms.[25]

In Aquinas's third argument, he says,

> A thing approaches the more perfectly to God's likeness, according as it is like him in more things. Now in God is goodness, and the outpouring of that goodness into other things. Therefore, the creature approaches more perfectly to God's likeness if it is not only good, but can also act for the goodness of other things, than if it were merely good in itself, even as that which both shines and enlightens is more like the sun than that which only shines. . . . Therefore, it was necessary that there be also different species of things, and consequently different degrees in things.[26]

It would be contrary to God's purpose of communicating his goodness to create only one type of creature. But in addition to creating a variety of creatures, it follows that God must include creatures that can act for the good of other creatures. This is because God's goodness includes acting for the good of other beings.

Next, Aquinas emphasizes something that has already been explained. He states,

> A plurality of goods is better than one finite good, since they contain this and more besides. Now all goodness of the creature is finite, for it fails of God's infinite goodness. Therefore, the universe of creatures, if they are of many degrees, is more perfect than if things were of but one degree. But it becomes the highest good to make what is best. Therefore, it was becoming that it should make many degrees of creatures.[27]

Again, God is intent on imbuing his goodness into creation, and it would be contrary to his purpose if he created only one creature. This entails that it would be fitting for God to create a great variety and diversity of creatures.

---

25. As mentioned earlier, Aquinas rejects the possibility of an actual infinite multitude (*ST* I, q. 7, a. 4). So, this would not entail that God must create an infinite number of forms.

26. *SCG* II, c. 45.

27. *SCG* II, c. 45.

However, although any world he creates will fall infinitely short of this goal, it would greater fulfill God's purpose to create a variety of creatures since a variety is better than only one.

Aquinas's fifth argument for the necessity of a hierarchy of beings is,

> The goodness of the species surpasses the good of the individual, even as the formal exceeds that which is material. Hence multitude of species adds more to the goodness of the universe than multitude of individuals in one species. Therefore, it concerns the perfection of the universe, that there be not only many individuals, but that there be also different species of things, and consequently different degrees in things.[28]

At *ST* I, q. 47, a. 2, Aquinas explains that if a species is incorruptible, there is no need for God to create more than one of its kind. God creates many individuals of corruptible species to ensure the preservation of the species. It would be insufficient to communicate God's goodness if he simply made one species. Instead, God must create a variety of species as well as a numerical abundance of individuals within each corruptible species.

Aquinas's next argument emphasizes God's intellect:

> Whatever acts by intellect reproduces the species of its intellect in the thing made, for thus an agent by art produces his like. Now God made the creature as an agent by intellect and not by a necessity of his nature, as we proved above. Therefore, the species of God's intellect is reproduced in the creature made by him. But an intellect that understands many things is not sufficiently reproduced in one only. Since, then, the divine intellect understands many things, as was proved in the first book, it reproduces itself more perfectly if it produces many creatures of all degrees than if it had produced one only.[29]

Because God is all-knowing, it would not be sufficient for him to simply create one type of creature. Instead, creating a large variety of creatures better communicates God's goodness. The product of an intelligent cause reflects the intellect of the cause. Just as an unsightly building shows that its architects are not good at their jobs, or a poorly designed building badly reflects the skills of its engineers, so would a universe with only one type of creature badly communicate God's goodness, which includes omniscience.

Aquinas's last argument says,

---

28. *SCG* II, c. 45; cf. *ST* I, q. 47, a. 2.
29. *SCG* II, c. 45; cf. *ST* I, q. 47, a. 1, ad1–2.

> Supreme perfection should not be wanting to a work made by the supremely good workman. Now the good of order among diverse things is better than any one of those things that are ordered taken by itself: for it is formal in respect of each as the perfection of the whole in respect of the parts. Therefore, it was unbecoming that the good of order should be wanting to God's work. Yet this good could not be if there were no diversity and inequality of creatures.[30]

Here Aquinas emphasizes that God cannot create a universe that would perfectly communicate God's goodness. Because God cannot create an infinitely perfect universe, God must perfectly order the universe to him. But an ordering would be impossible without the diversity and inequality of created things. Thus, God must create a universe with various grades and types of creatures.

To summarize, Aquinas provides seven brief arguments for the necessity (assuming God wills to create) of a hierarchy of beings:

1. As pure existence, God must create a world with diverse creatures because it is impossible for one species to represent his goodness.

2. As pure actuality, God must actualize a great diversity of forms to best communicate his goodness.

3. As loving, God must include creatures that are able to act for the good of others in the universe to better communicate his goodness.

4. Although it is impossible for God to ever create a world that will fully communicate his goodness, it is still better to include a great amount and diversity of creatures because more species of creatures is better than one species.

5. God must create a diversity of creatures because a diversity of forms is better than merely diversity of matter (diversity in matter only being necessary for the preservation of a corruptible species).

6. As all-knowing, God must actualize a great diversity of forms to best communicate his goodness.

7. The universe must include gradation and diversity to have order, which is necessary to show God's perfection (because God cannot perfectly communicate his perfection through an imperfect medium).

---

30. *SCG* II, c. 45; cf. *ST* I, q. 47, a. 2, ad1.

Animal Suffering and God's Purpose for the Universe

Implications for a Theistic Universe

These arguments have many implications for a theistic universe. It will be good to briefly discuss these implications to show what a theistic universe should include. This will help to show why arguments for naturalism from nonhuman animal suffering are mistaken.

First, it is good to remember Aquinas's concept that God must order the universe to God using a natural law. This entails that whatever universe God wills to create, it will be governed by physical laws. These laws will ensure that objects and organisms without intellects will fulfill their intended purposes in the universe.

Of course, a major implication from Aquinas's arguments at *SCG* II, c. 45 is that whatever world God chooses to create will include a great diversity and number of creatures. This entails that God must create a world with a hierarchy of beings. Aquinas explains this at *ST* I, q. 47, a. 2:

> Now, formal distinction always requires inequality, because as the Philosopher says (*Metaph.* viii, 10), the forms of things are like numbers in which species vary by addition or subtraction of unity. Hence in natural things species seem to be arranged in degrees; as the mixed things are more perfect than the elements, and plants than minerals, and animals than plants, and men than other animals; and in each of these one species is more perfect than others.

Here it must be remembered that existence and actuality are interchangeable with desirability and goodness. Implied within the concept of differing forms is the concept of inequality. The essence or form of a thing explains the actuality of the thing. When the forms of things differ, the actuality, and thus the goodness, of the things will differ as well. This of course results in inequality. So, if God must create a world with a large variety of forms, this necessarily entails that there will be a hierarchy of beings from the less perfect to the more perfect. Aquinas emphasizes that we see such a hierarchy in nature. There is an obvious hierarchy ranging from fundamental particles to elements, elements to plants, plants to nonhuman animals, and nonhuman animals to humans. In each case, the latter has more actuality, and thus more goodness, than the former.

This hierarchy entails something important for the current discussion. Contained within the concept of a hierarchy of beings is the principle that the lower creatures of the hierarchy exist for the good of the higher creatures. Aquinas explains this in the *ST* when he says,

> Now if we wish to assign an end to any whole, and to the parts of that whole, we shall find, first, that each and every part exists for the sake of its proper act, as the eye for the act of seeing; secondly, that less honorable parts exist for the more honorable, as the senses for the intellect, the lungs for the heart; and, thirdly, that all parts are for the perfection of the whole, as the matter for the form, since the parts are, as it were, the matter of the whole.[31]

Because the hierarchy of beings exists to communicate God's goodness, each species within the hierarchy exists for the perfection of the whole. Aquinas illustrates this by emphasizing the parts of human beings. Most vary in actuality and goodness, while all of the parts exist for the good of the complete human. Although the various parts possess unequal amounts of goodness, most are essential. Moreover, it would be detrimental if all of a human's parts possessed equal amounts of goodness. For example, the eye bestows the ability of sight to humans, while fingernails are not as important, although they also are conducive to survival. However, humans would be less good if they were simply a collection of eyes.

Also, each species within the hierarchy exists for the good of the species above it. Aquinas illustrates this when he emphasizes that the human intellect would be impossible without the senses, and the heart could not function without the lungs. This can also be seen in nature where plants are nourished by the soil, nonhuman animals are nourished by plants, and humans are nourished by both plants and nonhuman animals.

Another major implication of Aquinas's arguments is that because material things are corruptible, there will be a numerical abundance of each created species to ensure the survival of the species. Aquinas concludes from his arguments at *SCG* II, c. 45, and others, that God must include angels in creation. Aquinas believes that angels are immaterial, incorruptible beings who are pure form conjoined with an act of existing.[32]

As seen above, Aquinas argues that there need only be one of each type of incorruptible being. This is because their incorruptibility ensures their continued existence.[33] However, there must be a numerical abundance of corruptible creatures included in creation as a part of the necessary hierarchy of beings. This is obvious because if there are only one or two creatures

---

31. *ST* I, q. 65, a. 2.
32. *ST* I, q. 50, a. 1–2.

33. This is also because as immaterial beings without a material cause, it is impossible for there to be more than one number of each species of angel because there is nothing to numerically individuate one from another (*ST* I, q. 50, a. 2).

Animal Suffering and God's Purpose for the Universe

of any given species, the chances of their continued survival will be much smaller in a world with natural laws than the chances of a larger number of creatures of the same species.

Finally, an implication of Aquinas's arguments is that God must include creatures with rational intellects and wills in creation. This is seen in Aquinas's second and sixth arguments. God is pure actuality and all-knowing. Included in God's goodness is the ability to act for the good of others. So, if God wants to communicate his goodness, he must create beings that can act for the good of others and also create beings with rational intellects and wills (i.e., beings who are capable of understanding the communiqué).

To summarize, according to Thomism, a theistic universe should include a large number of differing types of creatures within it to fulfill God's purpose. This entails that there will be a hierarchy of beings with differing grades of perfection. The hierarchy should include beings that are both corruptible and incorruptible and should range all the way from the inanimate, to the animate, to the rational, and to the purely spiritual. Because the world is ordered with a natural law, there must be a numerical abundance of creatures within each corruptible species to ensure its survival. God's purpose is to communicate his goodness, so this entails that he must preserve the hierarchy of species, not necessarily individuals within each species.

Objections to the Arguments

Probably the most obvious objection to these arguments is that it seems that an all-good God would not include death and suffering in his creation. Death and suffering are evils an all-good, all-powerful, and all-knowing God should not allow. If God allows evil, then he cannot be said to be all-good.

The main point to remember in this regard is that Aquinas's definition of *all-good* is different from what most contemporary people will assume. As mentioned, Aquinas's definition of *all-good* mainly refers to God's infinite desirability and fullness of being. It is debatable whether Aquinas understood God's goodness to entail that God perfectly meets a certain set of moral obligations.[34] The main reason this is so involves Aquinas's concepts of God's simplicity and transcendence. Aquinas's arguments for

---

34. As mentioned, Brian Davies is a major proponent for the view that Aquinas's philosophy entails that God is not a moral agent. For example, see Davies, *Reality of God and the Problem of Evil*, 84–105.

God's existence entail that God is simple and is not composed of parts.[35] If God is simple, this entails that terms like *all-good*, *all-powerful*, and *all-knowing* are all different ways of describing one pure act of existence. Since these terms merely provide an analogical means of grasping God's infinite existence, Aquinas argues that we can never fully understand what they entail with our finite minds.[36]

As mentioned, Aquinas did not deny that God is moral. He emphasizes that we can attribute certain virtues to God such as truth, love, justice, prudence, and others. For example, "to love" for Aquinas is to will the good of the beloved.[37] Thus, God is loving because he wills the good of the universe and his creatures. Also, God is just (understood in terms of distributive justice) because he determines what each of his creatures should have and then ensures that they possess what he has determined. So, in terms of Aquinas's virtue theory of ethics, all of God's acts are good because they flow from God's infinite goodness.

But this does not entail that all of the moral rules that apply to humans are necessarily applicable to God.[38] We can know how God must act in some situations. For example, we can know that God is logically obligated to refrain from lying, murdering, and breaking covenants. He cannot do anything that would qualify as sin for humans because he cannot contradict his own eternal law, from which the moral law is derived.[39] But we could never fully know how he ought to act in every situation because to do so our finite minds would need to understand God's infinite actuality, which is impossible in this life.

So God is not necessarily obligated to eliminate evil completely as J. L. Mackie famously suggests.[40] Evil in the world does nothing to bring God's goodness into question because his goodness is essentially metaphysical goodness, not necessarily moral goodness understood in terms of what it

---

35. *ST* I, q. 3; *SCG* I, c. 16–28.

36. *ST* I, q. 12, a. 7.

37. *ST* I, q. 20, a. 2.

38. Laura Garcia provides a good discussion of the difficulties that even non-Thomistic philosophies face in the attempt to interpret God's moral perfection in terms of deontological, consequentialist, and virtue theories of ethics. She argues that virtue theories provide the least problematic interpretation of God's moral perfection (Garcia, "Moral Perfection," 221–32).

39. *ST* I-II, q. 79, a. 1.

40. Mackie, "Evil and Omnipotence," 201.

is for a human to be moral. But of course, the question of why God allows evil still remains.

To answer this question, it is important to remember why God wills to create. As stated many times, God's reason for creating is to communicate his goodness. This does not necessarily include keeping his creatures from harm or death. As mentioned, to better communicate his goodness, God must create a hierarchy of beings including corruptible and incorruptible beings. This entails that there needs to be a numerical abundance of corruptible beings within each species to ensure the survival of each species.

Aquinas discusses this in more places than just *SCG* II, c. 45. Right before his arguments for a hierarchy of beings, Aquinas explains,

> since the good of the whole is better than the good of each part, it does not befit the best maker to lessen the good of the whole in order to increase the good of some of the parts: thus a builder does not give to the foundation the goodness which he gives to the roof, lest he should make a house in ruins. Therefore, God, the maker of all, would not make the whole universe the best of its kind if he made all the parts equal, because many degrees of goodness would be wanting to the universe, and thus it would be imperfect.[41]

Here we see again the concept that a diversity of forms necessarily requires diverse grades of goodness in the universe. Just like a human made of eyes would be less perfect, so would the universe be less perfect if there were only one grade of goodness in it.

Another important point to remember is the Thomistic understanding of evil as the privation of good. Evil is understood as the privation of a good that should be present. As corruptible beings, nonhuman animals are naturally subject to death and suffering. Death and suffering may appear to be evil in that they are the privation of the ideal state of nonhuman animals. However, death and suffering are not evils because they are natural for corruptible beings. Thus, just as the lack of sight is not an evil for a rock, so also death and suffering by natural causes are not evil for contingent beings.

The natural corruptibility of contingent beings entails that the existence of death and suffering is not contrary to God's goodness. The existence of corruptible beings is necessary to accomplish God's purpose, and the nature of corruptible beings necessarily entails death and suffering. Even when God allows sentient and rational beings to flounder, this is an action that flows from his perfect love and justice. It is loving because God

41. *SCG* II, c. 44.

is willing the good of floundering creatures in that he wills them to exist and is just in that they possess the goodness that he has determined they should possess. But God cannot value the parts over the whole (including supernaturally endowing rational creatures with immortality) because this would contradict his purpose for creating. If sentient and rational creatures are immortal, there is no reason to create more than one of each. As already stated, such a world would not sufficiently manifest God's goodness. But if God could not sufficiently communicate his goodness, he would never decide to create. God's goodness is compatible with death and suffering because they are not evils for contingent creatures; they are not contrary to his purpose; and instead they are necessary for his purpose.

Here it might be objected that Aquinas's arguments do not account for all types of natural death and suffering found in nature.[42] It might be emphasized that some organisms are subjected to privations aside from the usual death and suffering associated with old age. As Draper says, there are a great number of organisms that "never flourish because they die before maturity."[43] Such cases involve abnormalities that are usually unexpected given Christian theism, such as birth defects, which cause organisms to die early deaths.

A problem with this objection is that it fails to realize what is involved with the natural decay of contingent organisms. When older organisms reproduce, this will many times produce progeny that possess birth defects, which result in offspring experiencing lives that are shorter and/or more difficult than their parents. If these offspring also reproduce, then defects are easily replicated within a population. Natural selection helps to cut down on the propagation of defects, but it usually does not fully eliminate them. Indeed, it would be strange for an objector to allow for natural aging and decay yet deny that this would entail birth defects and other complications. Thus, this objection adds nothing to what has already been discussed. For this objection to stand, it would be necessary to show that God is somehow obligated, logically or morally, to give organisms the ability to produce flawless offspring, regardless of the age of the parents.

---

42. I use the term *natural* here to refer to death and suffering that is caused solely by natural processes. This is opposed to death and suffering that is caused by the freely willed choices of rational beings.

43. Draper, "Christian Theism and Life on Earth," 312.

Animal Suffering and God's Purpose for the Universe

Implications for the Argument for Naturalism from Nonhuman Animal Suffering

It should now be apparent that Aquinas's arguments counter the argument for naturalism from nonhuman animal suffering. For sure, Aquinas would reject premise (2) of the argument that "the God of theism would more than likely create a world in which sentient creatures always flourish." On the contrary, Aquinas would endorse the opposite view that the God of theism must create a world that includes the floundering of sentient creatures.[44]

Draper argues that evolutionary theory provides evidence for naturalism over theism because "Darwinian explanations of good and evil are less complete when Darwin's theory is combined with theism than when it is combined with the no-design hypothesis."[45] Explanations of good and evil are less complete when they are combined with theism because they lack the knowledge of God's moral justifications. However, although many contemporary theists believe that God's perfection entails God is the most moral being in the universe (understood in terms of what it is for a human to be moral), we have seen that there is good reason to believe that this is not necessarily the case. But also, Aquinas's arguments show it is unnecessary to look for a moral explanation in God because the explanation is found in God's purpose for creating. And no moral explanation is needed because death and suffering are natural to contingent creatures. God includes these privations in creation in willing the perfection of the universe for the purpose of communicating his goodness.

Aquinas's philosophical theology and evil-as-privation view not only explain why God allows evil, but they also expose the explanatory inadequacy of the no-design hypothesis. Aquinas provides an objective definition of *evil*. It should be apparent that this basis is found in God. Evil is the privation of a good that ought to exist. This can only be an objective concept if the ought is derived from the form of a thing as determined by God. If there is no objective basis for how creatures ought to be, then theories such as the no-design hypothesis have no objective basis for defining *evil*. If sentient creatures exist for no reason, then there is no ought implied in their natures. Thus, the deaths of sentient creatures are not evils because their existence is not something that ought to obtain. Just like the lack of

---

44. Aquinas does not think that humans were naturally immortal before the Fall (*ST* I, q. 97, a. 1, ad3). This entails that all physical, sentient creatures in a theistic universe are subject to death and suffering.

45. Draper, "Darwin's Argument from Evil," 63.

sight in a rock is not an evil, blindness in a human would not be an evil if the existence of humans is accidental, and they were never meant to possess sight. For sentient creatures, existence and the lack of suffering are not objectively ideal states but can only be subjectively desirable states.

This lack of objectivity is especially relevant to Draper's concept that early deaths and birth defects count as evidence for the no-design hypothesis. If there is no objectively ideal state for any particular organism, there can be no objective basis for emphasizing concepts such as *early* deaths, birth *defects*, and failing to reach *maturity*. Indeed, words such as *early*, *defect*, and *maturity* can have no objective basis under the no-design hypothesis. If an evil is something that should not obtain, none of these things can be evils because there is nothing to objectively determine how long organisms ought to live or how their bodies should be configured. Thus, the argument for naturalism from nonhuman animal evil ceases to be a formal argument and instead is shown to be a mere statement of preference.

Moreover, theism offers more explanatory power in that it predicts the necessity of rational creatures and the floundering of contingent creatures. First, evolutionary theory provides evidence in favor of theism because evolutionary theory entails that the existence of rational creatures is highly unlikely. Thus, evolutionary theory combined with the no-design hypothesis renders the existence of rational creatures in the universe a cosmic accident. However, theism predicts the existence of rational beings in the universe and explains why they exist.

Second, Draper argues that "the fact that huge numbers of human and other sentient beings never flourish at all before death and countless others flourish only briefly, is extremely surprising given CT. It is not what one would expect to find in a living world created by the Christian God."[46] Aquinas's arguments for a hierarchy of beings show this to be mistaken in that floundering and death are not only unsurprising given Christian theism, but they are to be expected. On this view of Christian theism, floundering is expected because God should create a hierarchy of beings that includes contingent beings. Contingent organisms, by nature, are beings that will eventually undergo decay. The purpose of the hierarchy is to communicate God's goodness by pointing upwards to his metaphysical perfection. If the hierarchy contained only incorruptible creatures, this would not communicate his goodness as well as a hierarchy with contingent creatures.

---

46. Draper, "Christian Theism and Life on Earth," 313.

Also, there is nothing in God's purpose necessitating that he ensure all creatures live to a ripe, old age.

With these objections out of the way, in light of Aquinas's arguments for a hierarchy of beings, we should conclude that theism is more likely than naturalism if we assume, as Draper does in "Christian Theism and Life on Earth," that the antecedent probability of theism is equal to the probability of naturalism.[47] As shown, the no-design hypothesis has no objective basis for defining *good* and *evil*. The truth of evolutionary theory does nothing to confirm it. Thus, the probability of the no-design hypothesis is not increased in the slightest by the truth of evolutionary theory. Yet the truth of evolutionary theory would increase the probability of Christian theism. This is because Christian theism, as viewed by Aquinas, predicts that God will create a world that includes sentient and rational creatures that are subject to corruption and will inevitably flounder. Thus, the truth of evolution would confirm Aquinas's Christian theism by explaining how God causes differing species to arise in order to communicate God's goodness.

Conclusion

The argument for naturalism from nonhuman animal suffering states that naturalism is more likely to be true given the reality of evolutionary theory and the vast amount of floundering and death among nonhuman animals. The no-design hypothesis is said to be preferred because it is a better explanation for the evil found in our world. Moreover, the evil in the world also seems to be contrary to the concept of God according to traditional theism.

However, it was shown that this problem for theism can be answered through the thought of Thomas Aquinas who argued that theism entails the necessity of a hierarchy of beings. Aquinas concluded that the only reason God could have chosen to create is to communicate God's goodness. Also, Aquinas's philosophy entails that God's goodness is best understood as metaphysical goodness and not necessarily moral goodness. Given these concepts, Aquinas proposes seven arguments at *SCG* II, c. 45 that God must create a hierarchy of beings. These arguments conclude that God must create a formal abundance of beings in the world. This entails that there must be a hierarchy of creatures including both corruptible and incorruptible beings. The corruptibly of some beings, along with God's lawful ordering of the universe, entails that God will create a numerical abundance of

---

47. Draper, "Christian Theism and Life on Earth," 307.

Thomism and the Problem of Animal Suffering

creatures within their particular species. Also, God must include rational beings in his creation.

Aquinas's arguments and their implications expose the uselessness of the argument for naturalism from nonhuman animal suffering. They not only explain why God allows death and floundering (and predict that God will allow death and floundering), but they show how naturalism has no ability to explain what evil is. Also, they provide theism with the prediction that rational beings should exist in the universe. They render the no-design hypothesis explanatorily vacuous and entail that evolutionary theory provides confirmation of Christian theism. Thus, the evidence favors theism more than the no-design hypothesis.

All of this provides a holistic answer to Rowe's and Draper's arguments. Because God is infinite goodness and love, he created a universe to communicate his goodness. This universe must include natural laws and a hierarchy of beings, including naturally corruptible nonhuman animals. Nonhuman animals do not possess rationality and self-awareness because they are lower on the hierarchy than humans and, thus, exist for the good of humans. To maximize the survivability of each species of nonhuman animals, God bestows certain nonhuman animals with the ability to experience pain and suffering. Nonhuman animal pain and suffering is not evil because it improves nonhuman animal flourishing, and although it is unpleasant to its subjects, it is not morally significant for God to cause because nonhuman animals are not persons. For metaphysical and epistemological reasons, it cannot be known whether God is obligated to eliminate evil apart from special revelation, and the existence of evil is a natural part of a contingent world that falls infinitely short of God's infinite goodness.

Yet although Rowe's and Draper's arguments have been answered, there is another version of the problem of animal suffering that remains. This version is found in the writings of several young-earth creationists. In the next chapter, I will discuss this remaining problem and a Thomistic response to it.

5

Could a Good God Allow Death before the Fall?[1]

IN THE PREVIOUS CHAPTER, the final portion of a holistic solution to the problem of animal suffering (as presented by Rowe and Draper) was discussed. It was shown that classical theism entails a world created by God that contains a hierarchy of naturally corruptible contingent beings. However, there is at least one objection that might remain given this solution. Given that contingent creatures are naturally corruptible, does not God have the power to create a world with creatures that are supernaturally sustained in existence? Would not a hierarchy of immortal beings (beings that never die because they are supernaturally sustained by God) display God's goodness? If God is all-powerful and all-loving, should not he make a world that is initially free of pain and death? It might be surprising to some, but objections similar to these are mainly put forth by theists, particularly young-earth creationists.[2] Before examining their objections to a world

1. Almost in its entirety, this chapter was taken from Keltz, "Could a Good God Allow Death before the Fall?"

2. Young-earth creationists are Christians who believe Genesis 1 indicates that the world was created in six, literal, twenty-four-hour days. Young-earth creationists generally believe that Earth is between six thousand to ten thousand years old. This view is in contrast to old-earth creationists who often believe the earth is about 4.5 billion years old. There are several old-earth views including progressive creationism (the view that God progressively and supernaturally created different kinds of animal species throughout the earth's natural history) and evolutionary creationism (all life on earth is the result of the natural processes of evolution that were providentially guided by God). For a discussion of various interpretations of Genesis 1 by theologians, see Hagopian, *Genesis Debate*; and Charles, *Reading Genesis 1–2*. For a discussion of various views on God's use of evolution in creation, see Stump, *Four Views on Creation, Evolution, and Intelligent Design*.

Thomism and the Problem of Animal Suffering

that initially contains death and suffering, it will be good to discuss some background regarding the debate on this issue.

The intramural debate among evangelical Christians over the correct interpretation of Genesis 1 and the age of the earth has become heated at times. For example, in 2014 young-earth proponent Ken Ham attacked the credibility of the scientific apologetics ministry of Hugh Ross, an old-earth proponent. Soon after Ross released a book titled *Navigating Genesis: A Scientist's Journey through Genesis 1–11*, Ham included in a blog post that

> Dr. Ross misrepresents God to unbelievers by stuffing millions of years into the Bible and disconnecting death and suffering from its ultimate cause: man's sin. This does not encourage faith but suggests to them that God's Word is not trustworthy and damages the salvation message.[3]

Ham is adamant throughout his post that Ross's interpretation of Genesis can lead Christians to doubt the inerrancy of Scripture, undermines the gospel, and makes God responsible for creating evil.

Ham's claims led Deborah Haarsma, the president of BioLogos, to write a post on her blog emphasizing that the heated debate between Christians over the age of the earth is more to blame for young people leaving the church than the beliefs of the differing viewpoints.[4] Accordingly, Haarsma pleaded for "gracious dialogue" and invited Ham to a dinner with her and Ross. In response, Ham wrote a blog post in which he rejected Haarsma's invitation and likened the situation to when Nehemiah refused to meet with Sanballat and Geshem, who were maliciously trying to stop Nehemiah from finishing rebuilding the wall of the temple in Jerusalem (Neh 6).[5]

As indicated by Ham's comments towards Ross, young-earth proponents argue that a major problem with old-earth views is they seem to indicate that God created an imperfect world containing death, disease, pain, and suffering. Young-earth proponents say God would not only refrain from including natural evils in his creation, but also would never call such evils "very good." For example, in *Six Days: The Age of the Earth and the Decline of the Church*, Ham says,

> If you are a Christian and you believe in millions of years, you have to take all the death, disease, and suffering, and all the horrible

---

3. Ham, "Hugh Ross Twists the Bible to Fit Man's Fallible Opinions."
4. Haarsma, "Ken Ham, We Need a Better Conversation (Perhaps Over Dinner?)."
5. Ham, "Should I Have Dinner with BioLogos?"

Could a Good God Allow Death before the Fall?

things happening in the world, and you have to attribute these to God. If you accept millions of years, then you have to say, "Isn't God good? He calls death, suffering, and disease very good."[6]

What Ham is saying is that it would be terrible for God to create a world with disease, suffering, and death and call it "very good." Thus, any theist who believes that God did this should realize it entails that God is not good.

This argument from young-earth proponents seems to form a type of logical problem of evil concluding that God's moral perfection is not compatible with the existence of nonhuman animal suffering before Adam and Eve's first sin. To hold the beliefs that God is all-good, all-powerful, all-knowing, and that God created a world initially containing nonhuman animal suffering is to hold to a contradiction—or worse, to do so is to believe (knowingly or not) that God is not morally perfect. Since this is what many young-earth proponents believe, it is easy to see how the intramural debate can get heated.

Concerning the problem of animal suffering, it will be beneficial to philosophically examine this logical problem. The holistic solution to the problem of animal suffering presented in chapters 2 through 4 shows that nonhuman animal suffering is not problematic for classical theism. The solution entails several things regarding God's creation, but it does not cover the initial conditions of God's creation. If the logical problem posed by young-earth proponents seems to be insurmountable, then perhaps it should be time for old-earth proponents (and other theists who think the earth initially contained nonhuman animal death and suffering) to rethink their positions. If not, then perhaps young-earth proponents will realize that old-earth viewpoints do not necessarily entail that God is morally imperfect.

In this chapter, I will evaluate this logical problem involving death before the Fall. First, I will propose what I believe to be the formal structure of this logical problem. After listing the problem, I will discuss several theistic interpretations of God's moral perfection. This will help to clarify Thomas Aquinas's view of God's moral perfection and what it entails for the problem, although God's goodness has been mentioned in previous chapters. Before I further discuss Aquinas's view of God's moral perfection, I will argue that he could not have viewed God's moral perfection in terms of deontological and consequentialist theories of ethics. I will conclude that Aquinas's view of God's moral perfection is logically compatible with death before the Fall.

6. Ham, *Six Days*, 31.

The Logical Problem of Death before the Fall

As mentioned, young-earth proponents argue that it would contradict God's goodness for God to create a world that initially contains death, disease, and suffering. It seems that God's power, knowledge, and goodness should preclude the possibility of him creating a world that initially contains nonhuman animal suffering. Philip Ryken touches on this while discussing the importance for Christians to believe in a historical Adam:

> Are these natural disasters—the sufferings that some philosophers place under the category of natural evil—part of God's creative intent for his people? If so, then God would be open to the charge that he is the author of evil. To express the problem most provocatively, if Adam did not fall, then God did, by putting human beings into a world inimical to their survival... The historical Adam thus helps to explain human pain and suffering without attributing any failure to God. When we see "nature red in tooth and claw," as Alfred Tennyson described it, we are not seeing the world as it was meant to be, but as it became in consequence of Adam's sin.[7]

Ryken is saying the belief that God created a world that initially contained natural evils (before humanity's first sin) leads to the conclusion that God is morally imperfect (i.e., "Adam did not fall... God did"). This is because if God included natural evils in his initial creation, then it must have been his intent to subject humanity to disease, suffering, and death. Thus, if it is believed that natural evils existed before human sin, then it follows that the classical God of theism does not exist.

Accordingly, the young-earth problem involving natural evil in God's initial creation can be formulated as:

(1) God is omniscient, omnipotent, and morally perfect.

(2) A being who is omniscient, omnipotent, and morally perfect would not create a world that initially contains natural evil.

(3) God created a world that initially contained millions of years of animal pain, suffering, and death.

As mentioned, this is a logical problem for theists who hold that the earth is billions of years old and that animals existed for millions of years before humans arrived. Young-earth proponents would say these three propositions

---

7. Ryken, "We Cannot Understand the World of Our Faith Without Adam," 273.

together form a logical contradiction. The contradiction entails that there either could not be death before the Fall or that God is not morally perfect.

Of course, most old-earth proponents would not be willing to give up any of the attributes listed in proposition (1). So, this cannot be a proposition that old-earth proponents can target in the attempt to avoid the problem. Also, proposition (3) is not something old-earth proponents will want to give up either. Generally, old-earth proponents agree with contemporary science, holding that the earth is over 4.5 billion years old and that nonhuman animals were subjected to death, disease, and pain for the millions of years they have lived on the earth. To reject proposition (3), it seems that an old-earth proponent would need to deny the paleontological evidence suggesting that nonhuman animals have died for millions of years on the earth and instead hold that nonhuman animals, such as dinosaurs, were created alongside Adam and Eve. To my knowledge, there are no old-earth proponents who have done so. Thus, proposition (2) seems to be the only one that old-earth proponents can consider when attempting to avoid this problem.

Theistic Interpretations of God's Moral Perfection

This logical problem intuitively seems to be sound. But upon further consideration, it is not as clear as it initially appears. For example, the term *morally perfect* by itself is vague and can be understood in several different ways. As such, there are several different viewpoints regarding what it means to say that God is morally perfect. Because of this, the truth of proposition (2) is not clear and needs closer investigating.

Laura Garcia provides a good discussion of the various attempts that theists have made to explain God's goodness in the terms of differing ethical theories.[8] The three main types of ethical theories that theists have used in this way are consequentialist, deontological, and virtue theories. Each type of theory faces specific problems when applied to people and to God.

Consequentialist theories often view good actions as those that produce the best value for the agent and others who are affected by the agent's actions. An action is morally good if it produces the most value in relation to all available options. When applied to people, Garcia notes that consequentialist theories entail several problematic issues:

---

8. Garcia, "Moral Perfection," 221–32.

1. There is something odd about treating moral value as simply a function of non-moral value;
2. It is difficult if not impossible for a human agent to calculate the total effects of her actions in the short and long terms; and
3. It conflicts with our moral intuitions that we should be motivated by concern for others and their true welfare rather than by an attempt to calculate the optimistic action.[9]

Garcia says that some of the problems dissolve when consequentialism is applied to God.[10] For example, as a perfect and omniscient being, God knows the consequences of any actions he may choose to perform.

However, a major problem remains for consequentialism when applied to God, which is the problem of maximizing value. Some philosophers, including Aquinas, have argued that for any world God can create, God could have created a world with at least one more good thing in it.[11] If God cannot maximize the amount of good things in any particular world, then any world that God chooses to create will be a world that falls short of what he could have created. This entails that if God creates any particular world, he is not morally perfect because he failed to perform a maximally great action. This problem is known as the problem of no best world.[12]

Deontological theories view good actions as those that are based in certain foundational principles of obligation. An action is good if it is in accord with the foundational principles and bad if it is not. Philosophers have argued for various foundational principles, such as the Categorical Imperative, intuition, and divine commands.

Garcia notes that deontological theories entail several problematic issues when applied to people:

1. There can be cases of conflicting duties, where it seems one has a strong duty to do two (or more) actions that are incompatible with each other;
2. They place insufficient emphasis on the agent's motives and intentions in acting; and

9. Garcia, "Moral Perfection," 221–22.
10. Garcia, "Moral Perfection," 222.
11. For example, see *ST* I, q. 25, a. 6, ad3.
12. For a detailed discussion of this problem in relation to Aquinas's philosophy, see Keltz, "Aquinas and the Problem of No Best World," 503–19.

3. Since every good deed that exceeds what duty requires falls into this category, it is hard to say just how much extra good one must do in order to qualify as a really good person, much less a perfectly good person.[13]

When applied to God, these theories are less problematic in that if God is perfect, then he will be unable to fail in fulfilling all of his duties. However, a problem with applying deontological theories to God is that they only obligate creatures that have a choice in their actions. But in regard to any particular action, if God is only able to do the best action, then it seems that God is under no obligation regarding his actions, and moral perfection does not apply to him.

Instead of focusing on rules and consequences, virtue theories focus on the internal characteristics of agents, such as character traits, intentions, and motivations. Good actions should originate from an agent with valued internal characteristics. For example, an agent who has cultivated virtues such as prudence, justice, fortitude, temperance, etc., will perform good actions.

Garcia believes that virtue theories seem to be able to fix the problems that consequentialist and deontological theories face but mentions that virtue theory has its problems.[14] For example, virtue theory places value in virtues such as fortitude. However, there seems to be no way to attribute such values to God since it is impossible for God to be subject to pain or diversity.

Much more can be said regarding the implications and difficulties of applying these differing theories to God in addition to the discussion of Aquinas's views on God's goodness from chapters 2 and 4. However, a full explanation of this is not necessary because the problem regarding God and nonhuman animal death before the Fall is a logical problem. As such, all that is required to avoid the problem is to explain at least one way in which nonhuman animal death before the Fall and God's goodness do not entail a contradiction. However, it would be beneficial to discuss several reasons for why it seems that Aquinas did not understand God's moral perfection in terms of deontological and consequentialist theories. Understanding these reasons will help elucidate why Aquinas interpreted God's moral perfection in terms of a virtue theory.

---

13. Garcia, "Moral Perfection," 224.
14. Garcia, "Moral Perfection," 230.

Thomistic Concepts Precluding the Application of Deontological and Consequentialist Theories to God

Aquinas would not have understood God's moral perfection in terms of deontological theories. This is apparent in many places in his writings. First, as discussed in chapter 4, Aquinas argues that God created a moral law to guide God's creatures to their purpose for which God made them.[15] Everything in the universe is governed by God's providence.[16] Humans, as rational animals, are distinct in that they are not completely governed by physical laws. In addition to physical laws, they must be governed by moral laws so as to not override their free will.[17]

One striking aspect of the moral law is that it would not exist if God did not create it for the good of human beings. Aquinas believes that God's free will entails that God could have chosen not to create.[18] If God did not create a world, then this would entail he also would not have created a moral law. If there is no moral law, then it seems there would be no foundational principles of obligation that God could follow.

Indeed, Aquinas's understanding of what a law is seems to preclude the interpretation of God's moral perfection in terms of a deontological theory. For example, in the *Summa contra Gentiles*, Aquinas mentions,

> Since a law is nothing else than a reason of action, and the reason for everyone's action is his end, everyone who is capable of receiving a law must receive the law from the one who guides him to his end, even as the inferior craftsman is guided by the master-craftsman, and the soldier by the commander-in-chief. Now, the rational creature obtains his last end in God and from God, as we have already shown. Therefore, it was reasonable that a law should be given to men by God.[19]

Here Aquinas is emphasizing that a law is a rational plan of operation that is aimed at completing a purpose. A higher authority (e.g., a "master-craftsman" or the "commander-in-chief") bestows a law to a subject so as to guide the subject to the completion of the plan of operation.

---

15. *SCG* III, c. 114–15.
16. *ST* I, q. 103, a. 5; *SCG* III, c. 17–18; *De Veritate*, q. 5, a. 2.
17. *SCG* III, c. 114.
18. *ST* I, q. 19, a. 3; *SCG* I, c. 87–88.
19. *SCG* III, c. 114.

Aquinas mentions that only rational beings can be subject to moral laws because rational beings are uniquely able to determine their actions.[20] This might cause some to think that Aquinas could understand God as a moral agent in deontological terms. However, with Aquinas's concept of the term *law*, this is impossible because God would need to be subject to a "rational plan of operation" from a higher authority that is directing God to a certain purpose. However, there can be no higher authority in relation to God, for only God is infinite, perfect, and eternal. Also, there is no goal for which God aims outside of himself in order to perfect himself.[21] Aquinas argues that God must will God's own goodness, but there was no time at which God did not possess God's own goodness.[22] Although God's goodness is the object of his will, he has possessed his goodness from all eternity. Thus, there is no end at which God needs to aim so as to obtain some perfection that he does not possess.

Aquinas believes that, as pure act, God can only aim at one ultimate end.[23] Since this end is necessarily God's goodness, God cannot aim at any other end. This entails that even when God decides to create the universe, the end of the universe can only have God's goodness as its end.[24] And since God's goodness is the end of the world, even when God creates, he is not aiming at something that is different from his infinite goodness, which he has possessed from all eternity. Thus, God cannot be subject to any law because there is no authority above him, and there is nothing at which he could aim that he does not already possess. This eliminates the possibility of extracting an interpretation of God's moral perfection in deontological terms from Aquinas's writings.

Aquinas certainly would reject applying consequentialist theories to God. The main reason for this comes from his thought on God and best possible worlds. As mentioned above, consequentialist theories entail that a good action is one that produces the most value, in relation to other possible actions, for the largest number of people involved in the action. Applying this to God would entail that when God creates, he must create a world with the maximum amount of metaphysical and/or moral goodness/value.

20. *SCG* III, c. 111.
21. *SCG* I, c. 92; see also *ST* I, q. 19, a. 1, ad1.
22. *SCG* I, c. 80; see also *ST* I, q. 19, a. 3.
23. *SCG* I, c. 74.
24. *ST* I, q. 19, a. 2; *SCG* I, c. 86.

Thomism and the Problem of Animal Suffering

However, Aquinas does not believe that it is possible for God to create a world with a maximum amount of goodness. This is for at least two reasons. These include (1) Aquinas's argument that God cannot create something infinitely perfect because only God is infinitely perfect[25] and (2) Aquinas's arguments that God cannot create something that is actually infinite in magnitude or actually infinite in multitude.[26] If God cannot create an infinitely perfect world or a world that contains an infinite number of good things, then for any world that God creates, he could have created another world with at least one more good thing in it.[27]

This understanding that God cannot create a best possible world in terms of the amount of goodness is catastrophic for any attempt to explain God's moral perfection in terms of consequentialist theories. This is because consequentialist theories judge the goodness of actions based on how they relate to other possible actions. If God is morally perfect, then applying consequentialist theories to him entails that any world he creates should be the best possible world. But according to Aquinas, this is impossible, and there are an infinite number of worlds that are better than any world that God chooses to create. Thus, every possible act of creation is a morally wrong action for God. Even if God created a world with a potentially infinite number of happy people, this would still be an immoral action, which is absurd.

Garcia mentions that a possible solution to this is to say that perhaps good actions should be interpreted to be those that maximize the moral value of the world.[28] So, God would only be obligated to create a world with maximal moral value (i.e., a world in which everyone acts morally). However, Garcia mentions this is problematic because philosophers have argued it is impossible for God to know which actions free-willed creatures will choose.[29] If God has no control over what people will do, then the maximization problem remains.

Some Thomists have argued that God could create a world in which all humans choose only good actions.[30] So this is debatable within Thomism. Regardless, even if God could create a world with people who only choose

---

25. *SCG* II, c. 25; see also *ST* I, q. 47, a. 1.
26. *ST* I, q. 7, a. 3–4.
27. *ST* I, q. 25, a. 6, ad3.
28. Garcia, "Moral Perfection," 222.
29. Garcia, "Moral Perfection," 222.
30. For examples, see Davies, *Thomas Aquinas on God and Evil*, 4–5, 72–73; and Knasas, *Aquinas and the Cry of Rachel*, 214–25.

the good, this still breaks down into a maximization problem. This is because any world that God creates will have fewer moral people than an infinite number of worlds that God could have created. Even if God can ensure that everyone acts morally, he still must maximize the number of moral people, and this was already shown to be impossible according to Aquinas. Thus, for Aquinas, consequentialist theories are also insufficient to interpret God's moral perfection.

The Thomistic Concept of God's Moral Perfection

Recently, Thomistic philosopher Brian Davies has argued it is incorrect to interpret Aquinas as believing that God is a moral agent.[31] Among other things, Davies argues that God's simplicity, perfection, and transcendence entail we could never know how God should or should not act. In the *ST*, Aquinas seems to indicate that God has no moral obligations when he emphasizes,

> Since good as perceived by intellect is the object of the will, it is impossible for God to will anything but what His wisdom approves. This is, as it were, His law of justice, in accordance with which His will is right and just. Hence, what He does according to His will He does justly: as we do justly what we do according to law. But whereas law comes to us from some higher power, God is a law unto Himself.[32]

Here Aquinas is discussing God's justice and says that everything God does, God does justly because God acts in accord with God's perfect wisdom. Because God is perfect, so also his knowledge is perfect.[33] This entails that when God wills things, his knowledge, wisdom, and power are such that his effects will be exactly as he intends them to be. Thus, all of God's actions are perfect although there is no higher standard that determines what they should be. God is a law unto himself.

However, Aquinas's view of God's justice might not necessarily entail that God is not a moral agent. Thomistic philosopher Brian Shanley has argued in opposition to Davies and emphasizes that Aquinas believes certain virtues are attributable to God.[34] For example, in the *SCG*, Aquinas says,

---

31. See Davies, *Reality of God and the Problem of Evil*, 84–111; and Davies, *Thomas Aquinas on God and Evil*, 51–64.
32. *ST* I, q. 21, a. 1, ad2.
33. *ST* I, q. 14, a. 1; *SCG* I, c. 47; *De Veritate*, q. 2, a. 2; see also *SCG* II, c. 24.
34. Shanley, *Thomist Tradition*, 110–17.

> It follows, therefore, that the divine goodness contains in its own way all virtues. Therefore, none of them is ascribed as a habit to God as it is to us. For it is not befitting God to be good through something else added to him, but by his essence, for he is altogether simple. Nor does he act by anything added to his essence, since his action is his being, as we have shown. Therefore, his virtue is not a habit, but his essence.[35]

As mentioned in chapter 2, Aquinas is saying that because God is the source of all human virtues, the virtues must be in God in some way (or otherwise God would not be able to cause them). However, as Aquinas notes, "habits," as good or bad inclinations to an end,[36] cannot be in God as they are in humans. In other words, God is not called "good" because he tends to act properly, but because he is infinite goodness and infinitely perfect.[37]

Yet God could be understood as morally perfect in that he possesses certain virtues. At *SCG* I, c. 93, Aquinas says that the virtues of truth, justice, liberality, magnificence, prudence, and art can all be attributed to God. In the *ST*, Aquinas says that God loves all things because *to love* is to will the good of the beloved.[38] As mentioned in chapter 2, this entails that God's act of creating and sustaining the universe is an act of love. Elsewhere in the *ST*, Aquinas argues that God's act of creating and sustaining the universe is an act of perfect justice (understood as distributive justice) because God determines the good that each of God's creatures should possess and then ensures that they get what God has determined.[39] So the above quote, in which Aquinas mentions that God is a law unto himself, is not so much Aquinas saying that God does whatever God wants, like a theistic voluntarism, but that all of God's acts are perfectly just because they flow from God's perfect knowledge and wisdom. God's act of creating and sustaining the universe is also an act of perfect mercy and liberality.[40] It is liberal because God creates and sustains the world, not for his own use, but on account of his goodness. It is merciful in that God's creation and sustenance of the world removes the defect of nonexistence.

35. *SCG* I, c. 92.
36. *ST* I-II, q. 49, a. 1.
37. *ST* I, q. 6, a. 1; see also *SCG* I, c. 41.
38. *ST* I, q. 20, a. 2; *SCG* I, c. 91.
39. *ST* I, q. 21, a. 1; see also *SCG* I, c. 93.
40. *ST* I, q. 21, a. 3; *SCG* I, c. 93.

Thus, in a way, Aquinas believes that God is morally perfect because God possesses certain virtues and is ultimately the source of all human virtues. God's simplicity entails that he is his perfection, his love, his justice, and his mercy. So, God's actions will be performed perfectly, lovingly, justly, and mercifully. It is in this way that Aquinas possibly understands God to be a moral agent.

Regardless, as Davies emphasizes, it is impossible for human beings to know how God should act. As mentioned in chapter 2, at *SCG* I, c. 92, Aquinas notes that there are many virtues that cannot be attributed to God. These are the virtues of sobriety, chastity, temperance, continence, fortitude, magnanimity, gentleness, "and other like virtues" because these are associated with beings that possess bodies and passions. It is hard to see how Aquinas could view God as a moral being, at the top of the class of all moral beings in the universe, if two of the four cardinal virtues cannot be attributed to God. Indeed, it seems that Aquinas's doctrine of analogy is especially pertinent in regard to God's moral perfection in that there is something in God that is both similar to (i.e., analogous and not entirely different from) yet distinct from human moral perfections and, therefore, not fully comprehensible by finite intellects.

As mentioned, Garcia notes this difficulty for applying a virtue theory to God.[41] In regard to this problem, she suggests that this might not be a problem if love is understood as the source of all the virtues:

> On the positive side, virtue theories locate moral perfection in the will rather than in the intellect, treating right actions as those that are properly motivated and directed toward the right ends . . . This in turn suggests a more promising definition of divine moral perfection, understood not in terms of perfectly exemplifying the whole list of virtues but as exemplifying perfect love. If love is at the root of the human virtues, this definition has the further advantage of providing a clear analogy between human and divine moral goodness.[42]

Although many virtues cannot be attributed to God, he can be understood as morally perfect because he is infinite love. Thus, if it is noted that love is the root of all the human virtues, then perhaps God's love places him closer to a moral agent than Davies thinks.

---

41. Garcia, "Moral Perfection," 230.
42. Garcia, "Moral Perfection," 230.

However, it seems that Aquinas would disagree with Garcia on this. For example, when discussing God's love, Aquinas notes that it is possible to say that God loves some of God's creatures more than others. Aquinas mentions,

> Since to love a thing is to will it good, in a twofold way anything may be loved more, or less. In one way on the part of the act of the will itself, which is more or less intense. In this way God does not love some things more than others, because He loves all things by an act of the will that is one, simple, and always the same. In another way on the part of the good itself that a person wills for the beloved. In this way we are said to love that one more than another, for whom we will a greater good, though our will is not more intense. In this way we must needs say that God loves some things more than others.[43]

Garcia's solution seems to hold in that God's one simple act of will includes the creation and sustenance of creation. God loves all creatures equally considering this one act of will that is God's infinite goodness. However, Aquinas says there is a way to understand that God loves some of God's creatures more than others. This is when one creature possesses more good than another.

This concept has an interesting implication in regard to humans. Aquinas notes in the *ST* that it is proper to understand that God loves those who will be in heaven more than God loves the reprobate who will spend eternity in hell. Aquinas says, "God loves all men and all creatures, inasmuch as He wishes them all some good; but He does not wish every good to them all. So far, therefore, as He does not wish this particular good—namely, eternal life—He is said to hate or reprobate them."[44] Since God can be said to love some of his creatures more than others, when God reprobates some human beings, he loves them less than the blessed in heaven because he does not wish the reprobate to have blessed eternal life.

At this point, a helpful question to ask is, "If God's infinite love is the basis of all His actions, then why does He will that some people go to hell?" Aquinas says the answer to this question lies in God's justice, which as mentioned above, is determined by God's knowledge and wisdom: "it may be said of a just judge, that antecedently he wills all men to live; but consequently wills the murderer to be hanged. In the same way God antecedently wills all men to be saved, but consequently wills some to be damned, as

---

43. *ST* I, q. 20, a. 3; see *SCG* I, c. 91.
44. *ST* I, q. 23, a. 3, ad1.

His justice exacts."[45] In other words, Aquinas is saying that God's justice is the reason for why God loves some people more than others. But God's simplicity entails that God's justice is his essence. Elsewhere Aquinas accordingly says, "The reason for the predestination of some, and reprobation of others, must be sought for in the goodness of God. Thus He is said to have made all things through His goodness so that the divine goodness might be represented in things."[46] Aquinas suggests that it is fitting for God to reprobate some people as this demonstrates God's goodness more than if all were saved because it better demonstrates God's justice.[47] However, Aquinas says that we cannot presume to be certain as to why God chooses to predestine some and reprobate others. Thus, to understand God's reason for election would be to understand the divine essence. This is something that Aquinas says is impossible in this life.[48]

So, difficulties remain for interpreting God's moral perfection in terms of a virtue theory that focuses on love as the source of all human virtues. As mentioned in chapter 2, it seems that even if Aquinas did think God's virtues entail God is a moral agent, Aquinas held we could never know how God should act because to do so would be to comprehend God's essence, which is impossible. It seems Aquinas was content with reasoning to God's goodness through the workings of his Five Ways and metaphysical thought. God is infinite goodness because he is infinitely desirable and pure existence. This entails that God is infinite love, knowledge, wisdom, and power and, as mentioned, cannot fail to act perfectly, lovingly, justly, and mercifully. Although we cannot know how God ought to act, we do have a glimpse of what his goodness entails.

Implications for the Logical Problem of Death before the Fall

This Thomistic view of God's goodness has important implications for the logical problem of death before the Fall. As mentioned earlier, the old-earth theist must focus on proposition (2): "A being who is omniscient, omnipotent, and morally perfect would not create a world that initially contains

---

45. *ST* I, q. 19, a. 6, ad1; see also *De Veritate*, q. 23, a. 2
46. *ST* I, q. 23, a. 5, ad3.
47. *ST* I, q. 23, a. 5, ad3.
48. *ST* I, q. 12, a. 11; *SCG* III, c. 47–48; *De Veritate*, q. 10, a. 11.

natural evil." The solution concerning this proposition lies mainly in that God cannot be a moral agent in deontological or consequentialist terms.

First, it was shown that God cannot be understood as a moral agent in deontological terms. There is no principle that God must follow which would determine what he should create. This entails that there is no moral principle that God must follow that would preclude the possibility of him creating a world with nonhuman animal death before Adam and Eve's sin. Moreover, it was also mentioned that God's perfection entails he cannot fail to choose the best option in regard to any situation in which he makes a choice. This proves fatal to the possibility of applying a deontological theory to God's goodness because it entails that God is incapable of performing bad actions, and thus it would be meaningless to say he is obligated to perform certain actions.

Some might take this concept to entail that God cannot include death in his initial creation because to do so would be to choose a bad action. But again, it must be remembered that there can be no moral principles of obligation that bind God's actions. To say that God including death in his initial creation is to choose a bad action is to say that there is some principle that obligates God to exclude death from his initial creation. But it was already shown that there can be no basis for God to be accountable to moral principles according to Aquinas's philosophy.

Second, it was shown that God cannot be understood as a moral agent in consequentialist terms. Indeed, the above-quoted objections to death before the Fall from Ham and Ryken seem to assume an interpretation of God's goodness in consequentialist terms. But we have determined that there is good reason to believe that God cannot create a best possible world.

If God cannot create a best possible world, there will be an infinite number of worlds that will be better than any possible world that God decides to create. If this is so, and God is held to a consequentialist standard, then God should never create because every available choice as to which world to create is a bad choice because all involve a lesser amount of good for all involved in the act of creation. Thus, if God cannot create a best possible world, then it is absurd to hold him to a consequentialist standard since it is impossible for him to perform the best action in creating.

Here the objection considered at the beginning of the chapter might be raised: even if God cannot create a best possible world, then he should at least create a world without nonhuman animal death. However, it must be remembered that consequentialist theories entail that the goodness of

Could a Good God Allow Death before the Fall?

actions are based on the outcome of the actions in relation to other available options. This means that worlds without death are just as bad as worlds containing death because both lack an infinite number of metaphysical and moral goodness that God could have included in creation. A world with death might contain less metaphysical and moral goodness than a world without death, but both worlds are ultimately just as bad if they are lacking an infinite amount of goodness.

At this point, it will be good to mention another concept that Aquinas emphasizes regarding whether God has obligations as to what God can create. Aquinas argues that God is not morally obligated to nonexistent things. He says God is under no obligations or debts of justice to God's creatures in this way because God's creatures have nothing prior to existing.[49] Aquinas says,

> if we consider the divine goodness absolutely, we find nothing due in the creation of things. For in one way a thing is said to be due to someone on account of another person being referred to him, in that it is his duty to refer to himself that which he has received from that person. Thus it is due to a benefactor that he be thanked for his kindness, inasmuch as he who has received the kindness owes this to him. But this kind of due has no place in the creation of things, since there is nothing preexistent to which it can be competent to owe anything to God, nor does any favor of his preexist. In another way, something is said to be due to a thing in itself, since that which is required for a thing's perfection is necessarily due to it. Thus it is due to a man to have hands or strength, since without these he cannot be perfect. Now God's goodness needs nothing outside him for its perfection. Therefore, the production of creatures is not due to him by way of necessity.[50]

Aquinas means that God is not obligated to God's creatures prior to creation in at least two ways. One way an obligation can arise is based on the relation between two parties. For example, if someone receives goods or services from someone else, then payment or thanks are due. In this way, there can be no relation that would establish an obligation between God and his creatures when they do not exist. Another way in which obligations can arise is when something is due to a creature by virtue of what the creature is (i.e., what the creature ought to be according to its nature). For example, if God intends for humans to walk, then he is logically obligated

49. *ST* I, q. 21, a. 1; *SCG* II, c. 28–29.
50. *SCG* II, c. 28.

to create them with legs. However, in this way also there can be no relation that establishes an obligation between God and his creatures because God is not obligated to bestow goodness on that which does not exist. Thus, it is clear that there can be no deontological principle or consequentialist standard that prohibits God from creating a world that initially includes death.

Of course, showing that it is absurd to hold God to a deontological or consequentialist standard does not fully solve the logical problem. It still needs explaining as to how God's omniscience, omnipotence, and moral perfection are logically compatible with death before the Fall. So, what is left is to show that Aquinas's interpretation of God's goodness provides a solution to the problem.

As mentioned, Aquinas understood God as perfect and infinite in love, justice, and mercy. To avoid proposition (2) it must be shown that there is nothing unloving, unjust, or unmerciful in God's act of including death in his initial creation. First, as mentioned, there is love in God's act of the creation and sustenance of the world. Aquinas's definition of *love* as "willing the good of the beloved" entails that when God wills things to exist and sustains them in being, then God is loving them at each moment they exist. Also as mentioned, this is an act of infinite love because it involves God's one simple act of will.

Second, there is mercy and liberality in God's act of creating and sustaining the world. There is mercy in that God bestows existence and goodness to that which did not exist. There is the highest metaphysical gap between existence and nonexistence, and this entails that God's act of creation and sustenance of his creatures is an act of supreme mercy. Whether or not a world contains death does not eliminate the mercy from God's act of creation.

Also, there is liberality in God's act of creation and sustenance of the world. As mentioned, God is infinitely perfect and needs nothing to attain his perfection. Accordingly, God did not need to create anything and only did so in order to communicate his love and goodness to his creatures.[51] A world containing death also does not eliminate the liberality of God's act of creation.

However, it has been suggested that there are ways in which it can be understood that God loves his creatures in degrees. This concept seems to entail that there are degrees to God's mercy and liberality as well. For example, if one person goes to heaven, while another goes to eternal punishment, it seems that God loves the one that goes to heaven more and is

51. *SCG* I, c. 86.

more merciful and generous to that person than the one who is sent to eternal punishment. This might seem to be where Aquinas's notion of God's goodness fails to avoid proposition (2). However, God's perfection, justice, and wisdom are the remaining concepts that solve this issue. As mentioned, Aquinas believes that God created to communicate God's goodness and love to creatures. This was Aquinas's solution to why God would create although God needs nothing to attain perfection. As mentioned in chapter 4, following Pseudo-Dionysius, Aquinas believed that goodness is naturally diffusive.[52] So Aquinas argues that God decided to create because God was inclined, not obligated, to create rational beings who could understand God's goodness and freely will to be with God forever.[53]

God's purpose for creating has major implications for what he can include in his initial creation. One implication involves that it is not God's purpose to create a paradise for his creatures in which they are free from all harm. If this were God's purpose, then the existence of death in his creation would logically contradict his purpose and goodness. However, if it is logically possible for God to include death in his creation so as to accomplish his purpose, then this does not logically contradict his purpose and his goodness.

Aquinas mentions a logical possibility in this way in the *ST* when he emphasizes that lions could not exist if death were not a reality because lions feed on other animals by nature.[54] If God wants to communicate his goodness by creating a hierarchy of beings that demonstrate his power, knowledge, and wisdom, then it is possible that he would include lions in his creation. Indeed, as mentioned in chapter 4, Aquinas argues that God must create a hierarchy of beings in which the lower exist for the good of the higher if God wants to best communicate God's goodness.[55]

Another implication God's purpose has for his initial creation is that God must order his creation so as to ultimately fulfill its purpose.[56] As mentioned, God's perfection entails that there is no principle that obligates him to create the world in a perfect state. Moreover, obligations arise between parties only in situations in which both parties exist. Thus, whatever initial state in which God decides to create the universe will be logically compatible with his goodness as long as it is ordered to ultimately fulfill his purpose.

52. *ST* III, q. 1, a. 1; see also *ST* I, q. 19, a. 2.
53. *SCG* I, c. 86–87; *SCG* III, c. 25 and 37.
54. *ST* I, q. 22, a. 2, ad3; q. 48, a. 2.
55. *ST* I, q. 47, a. 1–2; *SCG* II, c. 45.
56. *ST* I, q. 103, a. 1; *SCG* III, c. 17.

God is only logically obligated to ensure that the world fulfills its purpose of communicating his love and goodness to his creatures. So, death in God's initial creation is not logically incompatible with this purpose and his goodness. Arguably, including death in his initial creation would better communicate God's goodness because it would better demonstrate his love, mercy, and justice. If death were a reality before Adam and Eve sinned, then this would demonstrate God's love and power to them better than if he had created them naturally immortal. When they saw nonhuman animal death, they would better understand God's care for them as God sustained them through their partaking from the Tree of Life. The reality of nonhuman animal death would demonstrate God's justice in that Adam and Eve would understand what their fate would entail if they disobeyed God. Finally, nonhuman animal death would demonstrate God's wisdom in that Adam and Eve would need to trust in God and depend on his wisdom so as to avoid their own deaths.

Conclusion

The claims of young-earth proponents regarding God's initial creation entail a logical problem concluding that God's goodness is incompatible with death before the Fall. This problem entails that it is logically contradictory to believe that God is all-good, all-knowing, and all-powerful yet created a world that initially contains evil.

To clarify the problem and also Aquinas's viewpoint on the matter, it was explained that there have been several theistic interpretations of God's goodness that involve deontological, consequentialist, and virtue theories of ethics. Each viewpoint has particular problems when applied to God in order to interpret what his moral perfection entails. In regard to Aquinas's philosophy, it has been shown that Aquinas could not have viewed God's moral perfection in terms of deontological and consequentialist theories. Deontological theories fail because there can be no authority above God to establish moral principles for him. Also, God is perfect and there has never been a time when he did not possess infinite perfection. So, it would be incoherent to apply guiding principles to God's perfect actions. Consequentialist theories fail in light of Aquinas's concepts that God cannot create an infinitely perfect world, an infinite world, and a best possible world. If there is no best world that God can create, it is absurd to apply a consequentialist standard to his actions and especially to his initial act of creating.

As mentioned, Aquinas's philosophy entails that God is all-good because God is infinitely perfect. All virtues are in God in a way because he is the source of human morality. However, many virtues that require a physical body cannot be attributed to God. Regardless, God cannot sin or will evil. His perfection entails that all his actions are performed perfectly, mercifully, justly, and lovingly. These suggest that God is a moral agent. However, even if Aquinas thought of God as a moral agent, Aquinas most certainly believed that we could never know what this entails for what God should or should not do. To know what God should do, it would be necessary to fully understand God's goodness, which is impossible.

Aquinas's understanding of God's moral perfection provides a possible solution to the logical problem of death before the Fall. If God cannot create a best possible world, then any world that he creates will lack an infinite amount of goodness that he could have included. However, God can still create because his act of creation is an act of love, mercy, justice, and liberality. Moreover, God is guiding the world to its purpose of communicating his goodness. It is not necessary to exclude death, disease, and suffering from a world with this purpose. Instead, it furthers God's purposes to do so.

This interpretation of God's moral perfection provides a solution to the logical problem of death before the Fall. Thus, it is wrong to believe there is no possible way that God would allow millions of years of non-human animal death, disease, and suffering before Adam and Eve sinned. God's goodness and the existence of death in God's initial creation are not logically contradictory. It is possible that God had a reason to include death in his initial creation that furthers his purpose for the world. Thus, old-earth viewpoints do not necessarily entail that God is morally imperfect.

The holistic solution to the problem of animal suffering from chapters 2 through 4 might have left some questions that need answering. Given that contingent creatures are naturally corruptible, does not God have the power to create a world with creatures that are supernaturally sustained in existence? Would not a hierarchy of immortal beings (beings that never die because they are supernaturally sustained by God) display God's goodness? If God is all-powerful and all-loving, should not he make a world that is initially free of pain and death? It was shown that the answer to these questions lies in God's goodness, the nature of a contingent creation, and God's purpose for creating. God is not morally obligated to anything that does not exist, including the world he decides to create. Moreover, God intends to create a world that communicates his love, justice, mercy, etc. God is not obligated to create a world that contains death (initially or otherwise), but such a world communicates his goodness more than a world that does not contain death.

Appendix

A Thomistic Answer to the Evil-God Challenge[1]

IN 2010, STEPHEN LAW proposed a challenge to theism he coined the *evil-god challenge*.[2,3] One of the central tenets of theism, Law emphasizes, is the *good-god hypothesis*, which says that God is all-good. However, Law believes that arguments for God's existence do not provide insight into God's moral character. Given this, Law says there is good reason to doubt that God is all-good as classical theism suggests. This is because, Law argues, theodicies (e.g., free-will, soul-making, etc.) that are often used to counter the problem of evil are not as useful as theists believe. Law proposes what is called the *evil-god hypothesis*, which is the idea that an omnipotent, omniscient, omnimalevolent god exists. Law says for every theodicy that is proposed against the problem of evil in support of the good-god hypothesis, there is an equally likely reverse theodicy that supports the evil-god hypothesis instead of the good-god hypothesis. This symmetry between theodicies and reverse theodicies, the *symmetry thesis*, forms the basis of the evil-god challenge. So, the evil-god challenge to theism is the argument that since an evil god is just as likely as the God of theism, there is no reason

1. Almost in its entirety, this chapter was taken from Keltz, "Thomistic Answer to the Evil-God Challenge."

2. Law, "Evil-God Challenge," 353–73.

3. Although Law coined the term *evil-god challenge*, several earlier philosophers have discussed similar arguments (as Law mentions in his article). See Madden and Hare, *Evil and the Concept of God*, 34; Cahn, "Cacodaemony," 69–73; Stein, "God, the Demon, and the Status of Theodicies," 163–67; New, "Antitheism: A Reflection," 36–43; Murphree, "Natural Theology: Theism or Antitheism?" 75–83; and Daniels, "God, Demon, Good, Evil," 177–81.

Appendix

to believe that theism is true over the evil-god hypothesis because theism includes the idea that God is all-good.

Since Law's article in 2010, there have been several attempts to explain why the evil-god challenge fails. Peter Forrest, Keith Ward, and Christopher Weaver have argued in various ways that it is either not likely or impossible that an omniscient and omnipotent being would or could be evil.[4] Anastasia Scrutton has argued we are pragmatically more epistemically justified in holding the good-god hypothesis over the evil-god hypothesis.[5] Most recently, Perry Hendricks has argued that skeptical theism sheds doubt on not only the problem of evil but also the problem of good and thus avoids Law's conclusion, which rests on the problem of good.[6] However, the debate continues as John Collins recently defended the evil-god challenge against recent objections and also extended the argument to theodicies not mentioned by Law.[7]

Although the evil-god challenge is not directly related to the problem of animal suffering, it will be good to discuss the challenge in relation to the theodicy proposed in this book. Accordingly, there are two arguments from Law and Collins in this debate that warrant closer consideration. One is Law's argument that semantic theodicies fall prey to the symmetry thesis, and the other is Collins's argument that the privation view of evil falls prey to the symmetry thesis. These arguments are interesting because, if combined, they would be opposing something similar to a solution to the problem of evil from the writings of Thomas Aquinas.

In this appendix, I will argue that classical theism, as understood and explained by Aquinas, does not fall prey to the symmetry thesis and answers the evil-god challenge. First, I will discuss Law's and Collins's arguments regarding semantic theodicies and the privation view of evil. After this, I will emphasize Thomistic concepts that were discussed in earlier chapters and used to answer the problem of evil, namely Aquinas's view of God's goodness and Aquinas's privation view of evil. Finally, I will show how these concepts relate to Law's and Collins's arguments and how these

---

4. Forrest, "Replying to the Anti-God Challenge," 35–43; Weaver, "Evilism, Moral Rationalism, and Reasons Internalism," 3–24; and Ward, "Evil-God Challenge—A Response," 43–49.

5. Scrutton, "Why Not Believe in an Evil God?" 345–60.

6. Hendricks, "Skeptical Theism and the Evil-God Challenge," 549–61.

7. Collins, "Evil-God Challenge: Extended and Defended," 85–109.

concepts avoid the symmetry thesis. I will conclude that Law's and Collins's arguments do not apply to Aquinas's classical theism.

Law and Collins on the Semantic and Evil-as-Privation Theodicies

In "The Evil-God Challenge," Law explains why various theodicies fall prey to the symmetry thesis and how they entail that theism is no more preferable than the evil-god hypothesis. One type of theodicy he mentions is what he calls the *semantic theodicy*:

> When we describe God as being 'good', the term means something different to what it means when applied to mere humans. This difference in meaning at least partly explains why a good god would do things that we would not call 'good' if done by us.[8]

Basically, semantic theodicies entail the concept that the term *good* is not used univocally of humans and God. Law mentions that a reverse semantic theodicy could be made by simply saying that whatever we mean by *evil* does not apply to an evil god in the same way as it does to humans.[9] Although it would seem that an evil god would not want to allow his creatures to be happy or healthy at all, this is not necessarily the case because the term *evil* applies differently to an evil god than it does to humans. This reverse semantic theodicy entails that good and evil in the world both equally serve as evidence for the God of theism and an evil god. Thus, the existence of the theistic God is no more probable than an evil god.

In "The Evil-God Challenge: Extended and Defended," Collins argues that the privation view of evil falls prey to the symmetry thesis.[10] Collins defines the *privation view of evil* as the belief that "Evil is held not to be something substantial, with positive existence in its own right, but rather it is the mere absence or corruption of substance or goodness."[11] Collins notes that although this view of evil is never proposed to be a theodicy, it does help theists to explain how God is not the direct cause or creator of evil. Regardless, Collins says the privation view of evil falls prey to the

---

8. Law, "Evil-God Challenge," 367.
9. Law, "Evil-God Challenge," 367–68.
10. Collins, "Evil-God Challenge: Extended and Defended," 87–89.
11. Collins, "Evil-God Challenge: Extended and Defended," 87.

symmetry thesis because a privation view of good can be formulated that is just as likely as the privation view of evil:

> The diabolist may avail herself of a similar argument for a privation theory of good, in which being is evil and good the absence of being. Note that Augustine says when a cure of the body or soul is effected, the evil—disease or wound in the body, vice in the soul—does not go away and dwell elsewhere. Poor as this argument is, it can be aped as follows: when a body becomes ill, or a soul becomes vicious, the body's health or the soul's virtue is not transferred elsewhere. The body is a substance, and thus something evil, and the goods are accidents, privations of the natural evil.[12]

Collins entertains a couple of objections to the privation view of good and argues they are no more successful in overcoming the privation view of good as are objections to the privation view of evil. Thus, Collins concludes, "Whatever the strengths and defects of the privation theory of good, they are paralleled by those of the privation theory of evil," and the privation view of evil falls prey to the symmetry thesis.[13] To understand why the classical theistic God of Aquinas avoids the evil-god challenge, it will first be necessary to recall Aquinas's concepts of God's goodness and the ontological status of evil.

Aquinas on God's Goodness

As mentioned throughout this book, Aquinas argues that from what we know about God from the Five Ways, we can know that God is infinite goodness. The result of Aquinas's arguments is something similar to the basis for the semantic theodicies that Law mentions, namely that when we say that God is "good," we mean something different from what we mean when we say that humans are "good."

As mentioned, Aquinas believes that goodness and being are interchangeable concepts in that something is good insofar as it is a perfect example of its kind. Since things in the world desire (or tend toward) their perfection, and since something is only perfect insofar as it exists as an ideal instance of its kind, being is interchangeable with goodness. Thus, the Five Ways lead to the conclusion that God is infinite being and, therefore, infinite goodness.

---

12. Collins, "Evil-God Challenge: Extended and Defended," 88.
13. Collins, "Evil-God Challenge: Extended and Defended," 89.

Also as mentioned, Aquinas argues that God can only be virtuous in terms of truth, justice, liberality, magnificence, prudence, and art. Since God is the source of all virtues, other virtues can only be in God eminently. Because God is simple and the source of all virtues, God is infinitely virtuous, but not in the same way as humans since God is infinite and perfect. God is infinitely virtuous, yet humans can never know what this entails for how he will act in any particular situation (unless he reveals what he will do) without knowing his essence, which is impossible.

Thus, Aquinas would agree that the term *good* does not mean the same thing when applied to God and to humans. Although we cannot know how God will act, we can know some things about what it means for God to be infinite goodness; God is infinite being, infinitely desirable, loving, and just. Humans are good insofar as they act virtuously and attain their perfection. Goodness is attributed to God and to humans analogously.

The Thomistic Privation View of Evil and the Problem of Evil

As mentioned in chapter 2, Aquinas held a privation view of evil. Following Augustine and Pseudo-Dionysius, Aquinas defines evil in the context of his understanding of the good:

> Now, we have said above that good is everything appetible, and thus, since every nature desires its own being and its own perfection, it must be said also that the being and the perfection of any nature is good. Hence it cannot be that evil signifies being, or any form or nature. Therefore it must be that by the name of evil is signified the absence of good. And this is what is meant by saying that *evil is neither a being nor a good*. For since being, as such, is good, the absence of one implies the absence of the other.[14]

When Aquinas says that "good is everything appetible," he is referring to his discussion of the nature of the good and the understanding that good and being are interchangeable.

The concept that something is only good insofar as it is a perfect example of its kind is what helps to clarify the privation view of evil. Evil is a privation because it is not good for something to be less perfect than it is intended to be. This is why Aquinas also mentions that "evil is the absence

14. *ST* I, q. 48, a. 1.

Appendix

of the good, which is natural and due to a thing."[15] So, evil is the lack of a good that ought to be in something.

This understanding of good and evil is important for Aquinas when discussing God's relation to evil. Aquinas has a high view of God's sovereignty and believes that because God is the creator and uncaused efficient cause of all things in existence at each moment they exist, God ultimately causes all things in the universe, even the free-willed choices of human beings.[16] With this view of God's sovereignty, it would seem that if evil occurs, then God could be said to be the direct cause of evil or that God wills evil for its own sake.[17] However, Aquinas argues that God does not will the evil in things, but instead God wills the good of everything in the universe while simultaneously willing the order of the universe, and evil sometimes results when good things come into contact with one another.[18] For example, God sustains lions and gazelles in existence, but lions eat (and cause the privation of goodness in) gazelles. In willing an ecosystem containing lions and gazelles, God is willing the good of the lions and gazelles and allowing the privations that occur when gazelles are eaten by lions.

Considering moral evil, Aquinas provides a similar answer. Although God ultimately causes everything in the universe, God does not directly cause the evil moral choices of humans:

> The effect of the deficient secondary cause is reduced to the first non-deficient cause as regards what it has of being and perfection, but not as regards what it has of defect; just as whatever there is of motion in the act of limping is caused by the motive power, whereas what there is of obliqueness in it does not come from the motive power, but from the curvature of the leg. And, likewise, whatever there is of being and action in a bad action, is reduced to God as the cause; whereas whatever defect is in it is not caused by God, but by the deficient secondary cause.[19]

Aquinas notes that an evil action is one that falls short of what it should be.[20] However, since God is infinite power and wisdom, his actions cannot

---

15. *ST* I, q. 49, a. 1; see *De Malo*, q. 1. a. 1.
16. *ST* I, q. 8, a. 3; *ST* I, q. 103, a. 5; *SCG* III, c. 64; *De Veritate*, q. 5.
17. *ST* I, q. 49, a. 2, arg. 2.
18. *ST* I, q. 49, a. 2; *SCG* I, c. 95; *SCG* II, c. 45; *SCG* III, c. 71.
19. *ST* I, q. 49, a. 2, ad2.
20. *ST* I, q. 49, a. 1–2; *SCG* I, c. 95.

possibly fall short of what he intends them to be.[21] Thus, the evil in evil moral choices comes not from God as primary cause, but from humans as deficient secondary causes.

Implications for the Evil-God Challenge

Returning to the evil-god challenge, it should now be apparent why Aquinas's concepts regarding God's goodness and the privation view of evil are pertinent to Law's and Collins's arguments. Aquinas argues that God does not will evil but allows it to occur as God simultaneously wills the good of his creatures and the order of the universe. When God and humans are said to be good in classical theism, this is not meant univocally. God is thought of as just and loving because he wills the good of his creatures at every moment they exist and guides them to him as their ultimate end. Death, sickness, and other evils are not willed by God for their own sake and are natural to contingent beings who depend on God for their existence at each moment. The notion that God ought to eliminate evil as far as he can is unprovable because we are not in the position to know how God ought to act.[22] Since we cannot know God's infinite goodness and how God should act, we cannot say that God *should* eliminate evil, and the occurrence of evil is not evidence against his existence. Basically, a Thomistic answer to the problem of evil is that God, who is infinite goodness, does not will evil for its own sake but allows it because certain evils are natural to the contingent creatures he sustains and guides to knowing and loving him. This position includes both a type of semantic theodicy and the privation view of evil. So, the question at this point is whether the Thomistic evil-as-privation view and the Thomistic semantic theodicy fall prey to the symmetry thesis. They do not.

First, the Thomistic semantic theodicy entails a deep asymmetry. This is because Aquinas's understanding of God's goodness is not a hypothesis. God's infinite goodness is a conclusion reached through the *a posteriori* reasoning of the Five Ways and the *a posteriori* notion that good and being are interchangeable.

---

21. *ST* I, q. 49, a. 2; *SCG* I, c. 95.

22. As mentioned, this is not the same as skeptical theism. Skeptical theists hold that we cannot know why God would allow evils in any given situation because we do not have epistemic access to God's infinite knowledge and wisdom. However, skeptical theism assumes that God would eliminate evil unless he has a good reason for allowing it.

Appendix

Recall that Law says we can postulate a reverse semantic theodicy, saying that whatever we mean by "evil" does not apply to an evil god in the same way as it does to humans. A reverse Thomistic semantic theodicy would be the belief that since God is infinite evil, we cannot know whether God should allow good, and therefore the existence of the good does not provide evidence against an evil god's existence. But Law's reverse semantic theodicy is not compatible with the privation view of good as Aquinas's semantic theodicy fits with the privation view of evil. This is because a privation view of good would entail that existence is undesirable, and nothingness is the ideal state of all things. However, for an evil god to be the grounding of all existence, an evil god would still need to be infinite in being without any limitations, as the Five Ways conclude. After reasoning to the cause of all contingent existence, the reverse theist would have no reason to say that God is infinite evil. This is because nothingness would be that which is desirable, yet an evil god would have unlimited being. An evil god would be infinitely undesirable yet would still be infinite goodness, not infinite evil. It would be incoherent to say that an evil god is infinite evil because an evil god is in fact infinite goodness.

Another incoherent aspect of a Thomistic evil god would be found in some of an evil god's vices. The Thomistic semantic theodicy entails that God's actions are loving, just, and liberal because God wills the good of his creatures and distributes goodness to his creatures exactly as he has determined. A reverse Thomistic theodicy would entail that an evil god is unjust in that he distributes being to his creatures although he has determined they should have no being. An evil god's actions are hateful in that he gives being to creatures because non-being is desirable. An evil god's hatefulness and unjustness might make sense at first, but considering that an evil god must also be ungenerous or greedy causes problems. As mentioned, Aquinas argues that God's actions are liberal because contingent creatures cannot exist by themselves. Since God is perfect, he has no need to create, yet nonetheless he bestows goodness to creatures. The reverse of liberality is ungenerosity or greediness. In the reverse Thomistic semantic theodicy, an evil god would be greedy with non-being because non-being is desirable. However, this reverse semantic theodicy would be asymmetrical because an evil god is infinite being, although non-being is desirable. Moreover, this reverse theodicy would be incoherent because it is impossible to be greedy with non-being.

A Thomistic Answer to the Evil-God Challenge

A reverse Thomistic semantic theodicy would also not work in that it would entail that *evil* as applied to an evil god means something analogous to *evil* as applied to humans. In a reverse theodicy, an evil god would desire the non-being of all his creatures because non-being is desirable. This would entail that to be analogously evil, all things would also need to desire non-being. But it was already shown that this is not what is found in nature. Human beings desire happiness and the perfection of their natures. They do not desire their destruction, sickness, ignorance, and unhappiness. Aquinas notes that even humans who make evil choices desire good things for themselves (e.g., other people's wealth, unnatural sexual pleasure, etc.).[23] If humans, by nature, desire being, this would mean that evil choices for humans would be those that bring about their destruction. *Evil* would not mean something analogous when applied to an evil god and humans because humans naturally desire being (it is against their nature and wrong to desire non-being), and an evil god desires non-being (an evil god never directly wills being). Thus, once again, the reverse Thomistic semantic theodicy would fail to be symmetrical because it would entail the false belief that *evil* analogously applies to humans and an evil god.

Collins's reverse theodicy fails also. It fails mainly because Collins does not understand Augustine's privation view of evil. Collins says, "The diabolist may avail herself of a similar argument for a privation theory of good, in which being is evil and good the absence of being."[24] However, it should be evident from the above discussion that this would be an incorrect view of a reverse privation view of evil (it certainly would be an incorrect view of Aquinas's evil-as-privation view). Simply calling being "evil" and non-being "good" does nothing to reverse the reasoning used to warrant the privation view of evil. Regarding the definition of *evil*, Aquinas says,

> good is, properly speaking, something real insofar as it is desirable, for the Philosopher in the *Ethics* says those who said that good is what all things desire defined it best. But we call what is contrary to good evil. And so evil is necessarily what is contrary to the desirable as such.[25]

If all things in nature tend toward their perfection in regard to fulfilling their natures, it does not matter if this is called "evil" or anything else. The concept would remain while only the labels would change because being

---

23. See *ST* II-I, q. 1, a. 7.
24. Collins, "The Evil-God Challenge: Extended and Defended," 88.
25. *De Malo*, q. 1, a. 1.

would still be desirable (yet called "evil"), and non-being would be undesirable (yet called "good"). Thus, as Collins has presented it, the privation view of good completely misses the mark as a reverse theodicy.

However, even with a correct understanding of the privation view of evil, it still does not fall prey to the symmetry thesis because of how Aquinas arrives at the belief that goodness is interchangeable with being. Aquinas argues that existence is desirable because all things tend toward and/or will their best existence. This view of being as desirable is an *a posteriori* position reached by observing nature. As mentioned, all things in nature, whether inanimate, animate, or rational, seek in their own ways their perfection.

A privation view of good would entail the belief that existence is undesirable. However, a privation view of good could only be warranted if inanimate, animate, and rational agents alike naturally tended toward and/or sought their destruction. But this is most definitely contrary to what is found in nature. Acorns always grow into healthy oak trees when unimpeded; animals always care for themselves and thrive when unimpeded; and humans always seek health and happiness. For the privation view of good to be warranted, there would need to be evidence that death, sickness, and, ultimately, nonexistence are the ideal states of all things in nature. It would need to be observed that everything in nature is perfect as far as it does not exist; fullness of being and health are privations of this ideal state. A world that warrants this view would be a world in which inanimate objects naturally do not exist or quickly self-destruct if they do exist. Plants would naturally be dead or sick if unimpeded, while only occasionally being healthy, if at all. Animals would seek their destruction and naturally be dead or sick if unimpeded, while only occasionally being healthy, if at all. Humans would naturally be dead or sick (with occasional health) and would desire to be dead, sick, ignorant, and unhappy. However, since it is obvious that the privation view of good is not warranted based on what we see in nature, a deep asymmetry holds regarding the Thomistic privation view of evil.

Moreover, aside from the warrantless nature of the privation view of good, it also would fail as a reverse theodicy. The Thomistic privation view of evil works because it shows that God only allows evil by directly willing the good of all creatures. However, since a privation view of good would entail that existence is undesirable, then it would be necessary to show that an evil god does not directly will the good of creatures. Yet if anything exists at all apart from an evil god, then it is unavoidable that an evil god is directly willing such a thing to exist, despite nonexistence being the ideal state. It would be impossible for an evil god to directly will the nonexistence of all creatures and, in doing so, occasionally allow them to experience privations of that ideal state. This is because if something does not exist, it cannot cause something else to exist. Thus, apart from its warrantless nature, the privation view of good is worthless as a reverse theodicy.

Conclusion

Law's evil-god challenge and Collins's extensions of the challenge may apply to versions of theism in which God is thought to exist only on the basis of design in the universe. However, the evil-god challenge is not a challenge to the God of Aquinas's classical theism. Aquinas's semantic theodicy entails that God is infinite goodness because God is infinite existence. Since God is infinitely good and transcendent, we can never know how he should act, and evil cannot serve as evidence against his existence. Aquinas's privation view of evil entails that evil is a privation of the good based on the observation that all things in nature tend toward and/or desire the perfection of their natures. Law's and Collins's reverse theodicies fail because of the *a posteriori* nature of Aquinas's conclusions. The privation view of good is unwarranted because it entails that all things desire non-being, although all things in nature desire being. Moreover, the privation view of good fails as a reverse theodicy because it cannot be said that evil god indirectly wills the good of creatures. Non-being is nothing. So, if an evil god wills the non-being of everything, then there would be no way for being to arise from the non-being of everything. These problems with the privation view of good alone render the reverse Thomistic semantic theodicy baseless. But the reverse Thomistic semantic theodicy also entails incoherencies in that an evil god would be considered infinitely evil, although he is infinite goodness, and an evil god would be greedy with non-being, although non-being cannot be horded. Similar to the privation view of good, the reverse Thomistic semantic theodicy also fails as a reverse theodicy because *evil* cannot be applied analogously to humans and an evil god. Thus, the evil-god challenge does not challenge Aquinas's classical theism because reverse versions of his privation view of evil and semantic theodicy are asymmetrical and incoherent.

Bibliography

Ahern, M. B. "The Nature of Evil." *Sophia* 5 (1966) 35–44.
———. "A Note on the Nature of Evil." *Sophia* 4 (1965) 17–25.
Allen, Colin. "Transitive Inference in Animals: Reasoning or Conditioned Associations?" In *Rational Animals?*, edited by Susan Hurley and Matthew Nudds, 175–86. New York: Oxford University Press, 2006.
Allen, Nicholas B., and Paul B. T. Badcock. "Darwinian Models of Depression: A Review of Evolutionary Accounts of Mood and Mood Disorders." *Progress in Neuro-Psychopharmacology & Biological Psychiatry* 30 (2006) 815–26.
Anders, Sherry, et al. "Depression as an Evolutionary Strategy for Defense Against Infection." *Brain, Behavior, and Immunity* 31 (2013) 9–22.
Andrews, Kristin. *The Animal Mind: An Introduction to the Philosophy of Animal Cognition*. New York: Routledge, 2015.
Andrews, Kristin, and Jacob Beck, eds. *The Routledge Handbook of Philosophy of Animal Minds*. New York: Routledge, 2018.
Anglin, Bill, and Stewart Goetz. "Evil Is Privation." *International Journal for Philosophy of Religion* 13 (1982) 3–12.
Aquinas, Thomas. *Aristotle's De Anima with the Commentary of St. Thomas Aquinas*. Translated by Kenelm Foster and Sylvester Humphries. Rare Masterpieces of Philosophy and Science. New Haven: Yale University Press, 1951.
———. *On Evil*. Edited by Brian Davies. Translated by Richard Regan. New York: Oxford University Press, 2003.
———. *Summa Contra Gentiles*. Translated by Laurence Shapcote. https://aquinas.cc/la/en/~SCG1.
———. *Summa Theologiae*. Edited by John Mortensen and Enrique Alarcón. Translated by Laurence Shapcote. https://aquinas.cc/la/en/~ST.I.
Arango-Muñoz, Santiago. "Two Levels of Metacognition." *Philosophia* 39 (2011) 71–82.
Aristotle. *Politics: A New Translation*. Translated by C. D. C. Reeves. Indianapolis: Hackett, 2017.
Augustine, Saint. *The City of God: Books I–VII*. Translated by Demetrius B. Zema and Gerald G. Walsh. Reprint, Washington, DC: The Catholic University of America Press, 2008.
———. *The City of God: Books VIII–XVI*. Translated by Gerald G. Walsh and Grace Monahan. Reprint, Washington, DC: The Catholic University of America Press, 2008.

Bibliography

Babb, Stephanie J., and Jonathan D. Crystal. "Episodic-Like Memory in the Rat." *Current Biology* 16 (2006) 1317–21.

Beck, Jacob. "Do Animals Engage in Conceptual Thought?" *Philosophy Compass* 7 (2012) 218–29.

Bekoff, Marc, et al., eds. *The Cognitive Animal: Empirical and Theoretical Perspectives on Animal Cognition*. Cambridge: Massachusetts Institute of Technology Press, 2002.

Bermúdez, José Luis. "Animal Reasoning and Proto-Logic." In *Rational Animals?*, edited by Susan Hurley and Matthew Nudds, 127–38. New York: Oxford University Press, 2006.

———. "Can Nonlinguistic Animals Think about Thinking?" In *The Routledge Handbook of Philosophy of Animal Minds*, edited by Kristin Andrews and Jacob Beck, 119–30. New York: Routledge, 2018.

———. "Mindreading in the Animal Kingdom." In *The Philosophy of Animal Minds*, edited by Robert W. Lurz, 145–61. New York: Cambridge University Press, 2009.

———. *Thinking Without Words*. New York: Oxford University Press, 2003.

Blaisdell, Aaron P., et al. "Causal Reasoning in Rats." *Science* 311 (2006) 1020–22.

Bonanno, George A., et al. "Sadness and Grief." In *Handbook of Emotions*, edited by Michael Lewis et al., 797–810. New York: Guilford, 2008.

Boyle, Matthew. "A Different Kind of Mind?" In *The Routledge Handbook of Philosophy of Animal Minds*, edited by Kristin Andrews and Jacob Beck, 109–18. New York: Routledge, 2018.

Cahn, Steven M. "Cacodaemony." *Analysis* 37 (1977) 69–73.

Call, Josep. "Descartes' Two Errors: Reason and Reflection in the Great Apes." In *Rational Animals?*, edited by Susan Hurley and Matthew Nudds, 219–34. New York: Oxford University Press, 2006.

———. "Inferences by Exclusion in the Great Apes: The Effect of Age and Species." *Animal Cognition* 9 (2006) 393–403.

Call, Josep, and Michael Tomasello. "Does the Chimpanzee Have a Theory of Mind? 30 Years Later." *Trends in Cognitive Science* 12 (2008) 187–92.

Carruthers, Peter. "Animal Minds Are Real, (Distinctively) Human Minds Are Not." *American Philosophical Quarterly* 50 (2013) 233–48.

———. "Meta-Cognition in Animals: A Skeptical Look." *Mind and Language* 23 (2008) 58–89.

Charles, J. Daryl, ed. *Reading Genesis 1–2: An Evangelical Conversation*. Peabody: Hendrickson, 2013.

Clark, John Spencer. *The Life and Letters of John Fiske*. Vol. 1. New York: Houghton Mifflin, 1917.

Clark, Stephen. *The Moral Status of Animals*. Oxford: Clarendon, 1977.

Clayton, Nicola S., and Anthony Dickinson. "Episodic-Like Memory During Cache Recovery by Scrub Jays." *Nature* 395 (1998) 272–74.

Clayton, N. S., et al. "Elements of Episodic-Like Memory in Animals." *Philosophical Transactions of the Royal Society: London B* 356 (2001) 1483–91.

Coleman, Kristine, and Peter J. Pierre. "Assessing Anxiety in Nonhuman Primates." *ILAR Journal* 55 (2014) 333–46.

Collins, John M. "The Evil-God Challenge: Extended and Defended." *Religious Studies* 55 (2019) 85–109.

Cory, Therese Scarpelli. *Aquinas on Human Self-Knowledge*. New York: Cambridge University Press, 2014.

Bibliography

Cottingham, John. "Decartes' Treatment of Animals." In *Descartes*, edited by John Cottingham, 225–33. New York: Oxford University Press, 1998.
Craig, A. D. "Interoception and Emotion: A Neuroanatomical Perspective." In *Handbook of Emotions*, edited by Michael Lewis et al., 272–89. 3rd ed. New York: Guilford, 2008.
———. "A New View of Pain as a Homeostatic Emotion." *Trends in Neurosciences* 26 (2003) 303–7.
Creegan, Nicola Hoggard. *Animal Suffering and the Problem of Evil*. New York: Oxford University Press, 2013.
Crook, Robyn J., et al. "Nociceptive Sensitization Reduces Predation Risk." *Current Biology* 24 (2014) 1121–25.
———. "Squid Have Nociceptors that Display Widespread Long-Term Sensitization and Spontaneous Activity after Bodily Injury." *The Journal of Neuroscience* 33 (2013) 10021–26.
Crummett, Dustin. "The Problem of Evil and the Suffering of Creeping Things." *International Journal for Philosophy of Religion* 82 (2017) 71–88.
Crystal, Jonathan D., et al. "Source Memory in the Rat." *Current Biology* 23 (2013) 387–91.
Curran, Kevin P., and Sreekanth H. Chlasani. "Serotonin Circuits and Anxiety: What Can Invertebrates Teach Us?" *Invertebrate Neuroscience* 12 (2012) 81–92.
Daniels, Charles B. "God, Demon, Good, Evil." *The Journal of Value Inquiry* 31 (1997) 177–81.
Darwin, Charles. *The Autobiography of Charles Darwin*. Edited by Nora Barlow. Vol. 29, *The Works of Charles Darwin*. Edited by Paul H. Barrett and R. B. Freeman. London: Routledge, 2016.
———. "Letter no. 1924." http://www.darwinproject.ac.uk/DCP-LETT-1924.
———. "Letter no. 2814." http://www.darwinproject.ac.uk/DCP-LETT-2814.
Davies, Brian. *The Reality of God and the Problem of Evil*. New York: Continuum, 2006.
———. *Thomas Aquinas on God and Evil*. New York: Oxford University Press, 2011.
Dawkins, Richard. *River Out of Eden: A Darwinian View of Life*. New York: Basic, 1995.
De Lillo, C., et al. "Transitive Choices by a Simple, Fully Connected, Backpropagation Neural Network: Implications for the Comparative Study of Transitive Inference." *Animal Cognition* 4 (2001) 61–68.
Descartes, René. *Discourse on Method and Meditations on First Philosophy*. Edited by David Weissman. New Haven: Yale University Press, 1996.
———. *The Philosophical Writings of Descartes*. Vol. 3, *The Correspondence*. Translated by John Cottingham et al. Reprint, New York: Cambridge University Press, 1997.
Dickinson, Anthony, and David Shanks. "Instrumental Action and Causal Representation." In *Causal Cognition: A Multidisciplinary Debate*, edited by Dan Sperber et al., 5–25. Oxford: Clarendon, 1995.
Dougherty, Trent. *The Problem of Animal Pain: A Theodicy for All Creatures Great and Small*. New York: Palgrave Macmillan, 2014.
Dougherty, Trent, and Justin P. McBrayer, eds. *Skeptical Theism: New Essays*. New York: Oxford University Press, 2014.
Draper, Paul. "Christian Theism and Life on Earth." In *The Blackwell Companion to Science and Christianity*, edited by J. B. Stump and Alan G. Padgett, 306–16. Chichester: Wiley-Blackwell, 2012.
———. "Cosmic Fine-Tuning and Terrestrial Suffering: Parallel Problems for Naturalism and Theism." *American Philosophical Quarterly* 41 (2004) 311–21.

Bibliography

———. "Darwin's Argument from Evil." In *Scientific Approaches to the Philosophy of Religion*, edited by Yujin Nagasawa, 49–70. New York: Palgrave Macmillan, 2012.

———. "Evolution and the Problem of Evil." In *Philosophy of Religion: An Anthology*, edited by Michael Rea and Louis P. Pojman, 271–82. 7th ed. Stamford: Cengage Learning, 2015.

———. "Pain and Pleasure: An Evidential Problem for Theists." *Noûs* 23 (1989) 331–50.

Dunnington, Kent. "The Problem with the Satan Hypothesis: Natural Evil and Fallen Angel Theodicies." *Sophia* 57 (2018) 265–74.

Eichenbaum, Howard, and Norbert Fortin. "Episodic Memory and the Hippocampus." *Current Directions in Psychological Science* 12 (2003) 53–57.

Epstein, Seymour. "Integration of the Cognitive and the Psychodynamic Unconscious." *American Psychologist* 49 (1994) 709–24.

Erdőhegyi, Ágnes, et al. "Dog-Logic: Inferential Reasoning in a Two-Way Choice Task and Its Restricted Use." *Animal Behaviour* 74 (2007) 725–37.

Evans, Jonathan St. B. T. *Thinking Twice: Two Minds in One Brain*. New York: Oxford University Press, 2010.

Evans, Jonathan St. B. T., and David E. Over. *Rationality and Reasoning*. Hove: Psychology, 1996.

Evans, Jonathan St. B. T., and Keith E. Stanovich. "Dual-Process Theories of Higher Cognition: Advancing the Debate." *Perspectives on Psychological Science* 8 (2013) 223–41.

Feeney, Miranda C., et al. "Mechanisms of What-Where-When Memory in Black-Capped Chickadees (Poecile atricapillus): Do Chickadees Remember 'When'?" *Journal of Comparative Psychology* 125 (2011) 308–16.

Fiske, John. *Outlines of Cosmic Philosophy Based on the Doctrine of Evolution with Criticisms on the Positive Philosophy*. Vol. 2. London: MacMillan, 1874.

Forrest, Peter. "Replying to the Anti-God Challenge: A God without Moral Character Acts Well." *Religious Studies* 48 (2012) 35–43.

Francescotti, Robert. "The Problem of Animal Pain and Suffering." In *The Blackwell Companion to the Problem of Evil*, edited by Justin P. McBrayer and Daniel Howard-Snyder, 113–27. Chichester: Wiley, 2013.

Frankish, Keith. "Dual-Process and Dual-System Theories of Reasoning." *Philosophy Compass* 5 (2010) 914–26.

Fujita, Kazuo. "Metamemory in Tufted Capuchin Monkeys (*Cebus apella*)." *Animal Cognition* 12 (2009) 575–85.

Ganella, Despina E., and Jee Hyun Kim. "Developmental Rodent Models of Fear and Anxiety: From Neurobiology to Pharmacology." *British Journal of Pharmacology* 171 (2014) 4556–74.

Garcia, Laura. "Moral Perfection." In *The Oxford Handbook of Philosophical Theology*, edited by Thomas P. Flint and Michael C. Rea, 217–38. New York: Oxford University Press, 2009.

Garrigou-Lagrange, R. *God, His Existence and His Nature: A Thomistic Solution of Certain Agnostic Antinomies*. Vol. 2. Translated by Dom Bede Rose. 5th ed. St. Louis: Herder, 1949.

Geach, P. T. "Good and Evil." *Analysis* 17 (1956) 33–42.

Gibson, A. Boyce. *The Philosophy of Descartes*. New York: Garland, 1987.

Bibliography

Gibson, William T., et al. "Behavioral Responses to a Repetitive Visual Threat Stimulus Express a Persistent State of Defensive Arousal in Drosophila." *Current Biology* 25 (2015) 1401–15.

Haarsma, Deborah. "Ken Ham, We Need a Better Conversation (Perhaps Over Dinner?)." *Biologos* (blog), October 13, 2014. https://biologos.org/articles/ken-ham-we-need-a-better-conversation-perhaps-over-dinner.

Hagopian, David G., ed. *The Genesis Debate: Three Views on the Days of Creation*. Mission Viejo: Crux, 2001.

Haldane, John. *Reasonable Faith*. New York: Routledge, 2010.

Ham, Ken. "Hugh Ross Twists the Bible to Fit Man's Fallible Opinions." *Answers in Genesis* (blog), September 27, 2014. https://answersingenesis.org/blogs/ken-ham/2014/09/27/hugh-ross-twists-the-bible-to-fit-mans-fallible-opinions/.

———. "Should I Have Dinner with BioLogos?" *Answers in Genesis* (blog), October 14, 2014. https://answersingenesis.org/blogs/ken-ham/2014/10/14/should-i-have-dinner-with-biologos/.

———. *Six Days: The Age of the Earth and the Decline of the Church*. Green Forest: Master, 2013.

Hamilton, Trevor James, et al. "Acute Fluoxetine Exposure Alters Crab Anxiety-Like Behaviour, but Not Aggressiveness." *Scientific Reports* 6 (2016). doi: 10.1038/srep19850.

Hampton, Robert R. "Multiple Demonstrations of Metacognition in Nonhumans: Converging Evidence or Multiple Mechanisms?" *Comparative Cognition and Behavior Reviews* 4 (2009) 17–28.

———. "Rhesus Monkeys Know When They Remember." *Proceedings of the National Academy of Sciences of the United States of America* 98 (2001) 5359–62.

Hampton, Robert R., and Bennett L. Schwartz. "Episodic Memory in Nonhumans: What, and Where, Is When?" *Current Opinion in Neurobiology* 14 (2004) 192–97.

Hare, R. M., and P. L. Gardiner. "Pain and Evil." *Aristotelian Society Supplementary Volume* 38 (1964) 91–124.

Harrison, Peter. "Descartes on Animals." *The Philosophical Quarterly* 42 (1992) 219–27.

———. "Do Animals Feel Pain?" *Philosophy* 66 (1991) 25–40.

———. "Theodicy and Animal Pain." *Philosophy* 46 (1989) 79–92.

Hauser, Marc D., and Laurie R. Santos. "The Evolutionary Ancestry of Our Knowledge of Tools: From Percepts to Concepts." In *Creations of the Mind: Theories of Artifacts and Their Representation*, edited by Eric Margolis and Stephen Laurence, 267–88. New York: Oxford University Press, 2007.

Hendricks, Perry. "Skeptical Theism and the Evil-God Challenge." *Religious Studies* 54 (2018) 549–61.

Heyes, C. M. "Reflections on Self-Recognition in Primates." *Animal Behaviour* 47 (1994) 909–19.

Hickson, Michael W. "A Brief History of Problems of Evil." In *The Blackwell Companion to the Problem of Evil*, edited by Justin P. McBrayer and Daniel Howard-Snyder, 3–18. Chichester: Wiley-Blackwell, 2013.

Hull, David L. "The God of the Galápagos." *Nature* 352 (1991) 485–86.

Hume, David. *Dialogues Concerning Natural Religion and Other Writings*. Edited by Dorothy Coleman. Cambridge: Cambridge University Press, 2007.

Huntley, William B. "David Hume and Charles Darwin." *Journal of the History of Ideas* 33 (1972) 457–70.

Bibliography

Hurley, Susan, and Matthew Nudds, eds. *Rational Animals?* New York: Oxford University Press, 2006.

Jozefowiez, J., et al. "Metacognition in Animals: How Do We Know that They Know?" *Comparative Cognition and Behavior Reviews* 4 (2009) 29–39.

Kacelnik, Alex. "Meanings of Rationality." In *Rational Animals?*, edited by Susan Hurley and Matthew Nudds, 87–106. New York: Oxford University Press, 2006.

Kane, G. Stanley. "Evil and Privation." *International Journal for Philosophy of Religion* 11 (1980) 43–58.

Keltner, Dacher, and Ann M. Kring. "Emotion, Social Function, and Psychopathology." *Review of General Psychology* 2 (1998) 320–42.

Keltz, B. Kyle. "Aquinas and the Problem of No Best World." *New Blackfriars* 99 (2018) 503–19.

———. "Could a Good God Allow Death before the Fall? A Thomistic Perspective." *The Heythrop Journal* (2017). doi: 10.1111/heyj.12658.

———. "God's Purpose for the Universe and the Problem of Animal Suffering." *Sophia* 59 (2019) 475–92.

———. "Is Animal Suffering Evil? A Thomistic Perspective." *The Journal of Value Inquiry* 54 (2020) 1–19.

———. "A Thomistic Answer to the Evil-God Challenge." *The Heythrop Journal* 60 (2019) 689–98.

———. "Neo-Thomism and the Problem of Animal Suffering." *Nova et Vetera* 17 (2019) 93–125.

Keren, Gideon, and Yaacov Schul. "Two Is Not Always Better Than One: A Critical Evaluation of Two-System Theories." *Perspectives on Psychological Science* 4 (2009) 533–50.

King, Peter. "Emotions." In *The Oxford Handbook of Aquinas*, edited by Brian Davies and Eleonore Stump, 209–26. New York: Oxford University Press, 2012.

Klein, Colin. *What the Body Commands: The Imperative Theory of Pain*. Cambridge: Massachusetts Institute of Technology Press, 2015.

Knasas, John F. X. *Aquinas and the Cry of Rachel: Thomistic Reflections on the Problem of Evil*. Washington, DC: The Catholic University of America Press, 2013.

Kornell, Nate, et al. "Transfer of Metacognitive Skill and Hint Seeking in Monkeys." *Psychological Science* 18 (2007) 64–71.

Kretzmann, Norman. *The Metaphysics of Creation: Aquinas's Natural Theology in Summa Contra Gentiles II*. Oxford: Clarendon, 1999.

Kruglanski, Arie W., and Edward Orehek. "Partitioning the Domain of Social Inference: Dual Mode and Systems Models and Their Alternatives." *Annual Review of Psychology* 58 (2007) 291–316.

Kruglanski, Arie W., and Gerd Gigerenzer. "Intuitive and Deliberate Judgments Are Based on Common Principles." *Psychological Review* 118 (2011) 97–109.

Kruglanski, Arie W., et al. "A Parametric Unimodel of Human Judgment: Integrating Dual-Process Frameworks in Social Cognition from a Single-Mode Perspective." In *Social Judgments: Implicit and Explicit Processes*, edited by Joseph P. Forgas et al., 137–61. New York: Cambridge University Press, 2003.

Lang, Peter J., et al. "Fear and Anxiety: Animal Models and Human Cognitive Psychophysiology." *Journal of Affective Disorders* 61 (2000) 137–59.

Law, Stephen. "The Evil-God Challenge." *Religious Studies* 46 (2010) 353–73.

Lazarus, Richard S. *Emotion and Adaptation*. New York: Oxford University Press, 1991.

Bibliography

Le Pelley, M. E. "Metacognitive Monkeys or Associative Animals? Simple Reinforcement Learning Explains Uncertainty in Nonhuman Animals." *Journal of Experimental Psychology: Learning, Memory, and Cognition* 38 (2012) 686-708.

Lewis, C. S. *The Problem of Pain*. Reprint, New York: HarperOne, 2001.

Lewis, Michael, et al., eds. *Handbook of Emotions*. 3rd ed. New York: Guilford, 2008.

Lind, Johan. "What Can Associative Learning Do for Planning?" *Royal Society Open Science* 5 (2018) 1-14. doi: 10.1098/rsos.180778.

Loeser, J. D. "Perspectives on Pain." In *Clinical Pharmacology & Therapeutics*, edited by P. Turner et al., 313-16. New York: MacMillan, 1980.

Lynch, Joseph J. "Harrison and Hick on God and Animal Pain." *Sophia* 33 (1994) 62-73.

Mackie, J. L. "Evil and Omnipotence." *Mind* 64 (1955) 200-212.

Madden, Edward H., and Peter H. Hare. *Evil and the Concept of God*. Springfield: Thomas, 1968.

Marchand, Serge. *The Phenomenon of Pain*. Seattle: International Association for the Study of Pain, 2012.

Markowitsch, Hans J., and Angelica Staniloiu. "Memory, Autonoetic Consciousness, and the Self." *Consciousness and Cognition* 20 (2011) 16-39.

Martin-Ordas, Gema, et al. "Keeping Track of Time: Evidence for Episodic-Like Memory in Great Apes." *Animal Cognition* 13 (2010) 331-40.

Martinez, Manolo. "Imperative Content and the Painfulness of Pain." *Phenomenology and the Cognitive Sciences* 10 (2011) 67-90.

Mawson, T. J. Review of *Nature Red in Tooth and Claw: Theism and the Problem of Animal Suffering*, by Michael Murray. *Mind* 118 (2009) 855-58.

McBrayer, Justin P. "Skeptical Theism." *Philosophy Compass* 5 (2010) 611-23.

McBrayer, Justin P., and Daniel Howard-Snyder, eds. *The Blackwell Companion to the Problem of Evil*. Chichester: Wiley, 2013.

McGonigle, Brendan O., and Margaret Chalmers. "Are Monkeys Logical?" *Nature* 267 (1977) 694-96.

———. "Monkeys Are Rational!" *The Quarterly Journal of Social Knowledge in Monkeys* 45B (1992) 198-228.

Melzack, Ronald, and Patrick D. Wall. *The Challenge of Pain*. 2nd ed. New York: Penguin, 2008.

Metcalfe, Janet, and Lisa K. Son. "Anoetic, Noetic, and Autonoetic Metacognition." In *Foundations of Metacognition*, edited by Michael J. Beran et al., 289-301. New York: Oxford University Press, 2012.

More, Henry. "More to Descartes, 11 December 1648." In *Oeuvres de Descartes*, edited by Charles Adam and Paul Tannery, 5:235-50. Paris: Léopold Cerf, 1903.

Murphree, Wallace A. "Natural Theology: Theism or Antitheism?" *Sophia* 36 (1997) 75-83.

Murray, Michael J. *Nature Red in Tooth and Claw: Theism and the Problem of Animal Suffering*. New York: Oxford University Press, 2008.

———. Review of *The Problem of Animal Pain: A Theodicy for All Creatures Great and Small*, by Trent Dougherty. *International Journal for Philosophy of Religion* 78 (2015) 137-41.

Murray, Michael J., and Glenn Ross. "Neo-Cartesianism and the Problem of Animal Suffering." *Faith and Philosophy* 23 (2006) 169-90.

Nagasako, Elna M., et al. "Congenital Insensitivity to Pain: An Update." *Pain* 101 (2003) 213-19.

New, Christopher. "Antitheism: A Reflection." *Ratio* 6 (1993) 36-43.

Bibliography

Öhman, Arne, and Susan Mineka. "Fears, Phobias, and Preparedness: Toward an Evolved Module of Fear and Fear Learning." *Psychological Review* 108 (2001) 483–522.

Oppy, Graham. "Rowe's Evidential Arguments from Evil." In *The Blackwell Companion to the Problem of Evil*, edited by Justin P. McBrayer and Daniel Howard-Snyder, 49–66. Chichester: Wiley, 2013.

Osman, Magda. "An Evaluation of Dual-Process Theories of Reasoning." *Psychonomic Bulletin and Review* 11 (2004) 988–1010.

Penn, Derek C., and Daniel J. Povinelli. "Causal Cognition in Human and Nonhuman Animals: A Comparative, Critical Review." *Annual Review of Psychology* 58 (2007) 97–118.

Penn, Derek C., et al. "Darwin's Mistake: Explaining the Discontinuity Between Human and Nonhuman Minds." *Behavioral and Brain Sciences* 31 (2008) 109–30.

Perrot-Minnot, Marie-Jeanne, et al. "Anxiety-Like Behaviour Increases Safety from Fish Predation in an Amphipod Crustacea." *Royal Society Open Science* 4 (2017). doi: 10.1098/rsos.171558.

Povinelli, Daniel J., and Jennifer Vonk. "Chimpanzee Minds: Suspiciously Human?" *Trends in Cognitive Sciences* 7 (2003) 157–60.

———. "We Don't Need a Microscope." In *Rational Animals?*, edited by Susan Hurley and Matthew Nudds, 385–412. New York: Oxford University Press, 2006.

Proust, Joëlle. "Metacognition." *Philosophy Compass* 5 (2010) 989–98.

Rescorla, Michael. "Cognitive Maps and the Language of Thought." *The British Journal for the Philosophy of Science* 60 (2009) 377–407.

Roberts, William A. "Are Animals Stuck in Time?" *Psychological Bulletin* 128 (2002) 473–89.

Robson, Mark Ian Thomas. "Evil, Privation, Depression and Dread." *New Blackfriars* 94 (2013) 552–64.

Rolls, Edmund T. *Emotion and Decision-Making Explained*. New York: Oxford University Press, 2014.

Rosenbaum, R. Shayna, et al. "The Case of K.C.: Contributions of a Memory-Impaired Person to Memory Theory." *Neuropsychologia* 43 (2005) 989–1021.

Rowe, William L. "The Problem of Evil and Some Varieties of Atheism." *American Philosophical Quarterly* 16 (1979) 335–41.

Russell, Bertrand. *Religion and Science*. Reprint, New York: Oxford University Press, 2011.

Ryken, Philip G. "We Cannot Understand the World of Our Faith Without a Real, Historical Adam." In *Four Views of the Historical Adam*, edited by Matthew Barrett and Ardel B. Caneday, 267–79. Grand Rapids: Zondervan, 2013.

Schusterman, Ronald J., et al. "The Cognitive Sea Lion: Meaning and Memory in the Laboratory and in Nature." In *The Cognitive Animal: Empirical and Theoretical Perspectives on Animal Cognition*, edited by Marc Bekoff et al., 217–28. Cambridge: Massachusetts Institute of Technology Press, 2002.

Schwarz, Norbert. "Warmer and More Social: Recent Developments in Cognitive Social Psychology." *Annual Review of Sociology* 24 (1998) 239–64.

Scrutton, Anastasia Phillippa. "Why Not Believe in an Evil God? Pragmatic Encroachment and Some Implications for Philosophy of Religion." *Religious Studies* 52 (2016) 345–60.

Seyfarth, Robert M., and Dorothy L. Cheney. "The Structure of Social Knowledge in Monkeys." In *The Cognitive Animal: Empirical and Theoretical Perspectives on Animal Cognition*, edited by Marc Bekoff et al., 379–84. Cambridge: Massachusetts Institute of Technology Press, 2002.

Bibliography

Shanley, Brian J. *The Thomist Tradition*. Dordrecht: Kluwer Academic, 2002.
Shields, Wendy E., et al. "Uncertain Responses by Humans and Rhesus Monkeys (*Macaca mulatta*) in a Psychophysical Same-Different Task." *Journal of Experimental Psychology: General* 126 (1997) 147–64.
Smith, Eliot R., and Jamie DeCoster. "Dual-Process Models in Social and Cognitive Psychology: Conceptual Integration and Links to Underlying Memory Systems." *Personality and Social Psychology Review* 4 (2000) 108–31.
Smith, J. David. "The Study of Animal Metacognition." *Trends in Cognitive Sciences* 13 (2009) 389–96.
Smith, J. David, et al. "Dissociating Uncertainty Responses and Reinforcement Signals in the Comparative Study of Uncertainty Monitoring." *Journal of Experimental Psychology: General* 135 (2006) 282–97.
Smith, Norman Kemp. *New Studies in the Philosophy of Descartes*. New York: Russell & Russell, 1963.
Smith, Quentin. "An Atheological Argument from Evil Natural Laws." *International Journal for Philosophy of Religion* 29 (1991) 159–74.
Southgate, Christopher. *The Groaning of Creation: God, Evolution, and the Problem of Evil*. Louisville: Westminster John Knox, 2008.
Speak, Daniel. "Free Will and Soul-Making Theodicies." In *The Blackwell Companion to the Problem of Evil*, edited by Justin P. McBrayer and Daniel Howard-Snyder, 205–21. Chichester: Wiley-Blackwell, 2013.
Stanovich, Keith E. *Rationality and the Reflective Mind*. New York: Oxford University Press, 2011.
Stein, Edward. "God, the Demon, and the Status of Theodicies." *American Philosophical Quarterly* 27 (1990) 163–67.
Steiner, Gary. *Anthropocentrism and Its Discontents: The Moral Status of Animals in the History of Western Philosophy*. Reprint, Pittsburgh: University of Pittsburgh Press, 2010.
———. "Descartes, Christianity, and Contemporary Speciesism." In *A Communion of Subjects: Animals in Religion, Science, and Ethics*, edited by Paul Waldau and Kimberly Patton, 117–31. New York: Columbia University Press, 2006.
Stewart, Adam, et al. "Modeling Anxiety Using Adult Zebrafish: A Conceptual Review." *Neuropharmacology* 62 (2012) 135–43.
Stump, Eleonore. *Aquinas*. New York: Routledge, 2003.
Stump, J. B. *Four Views on Creation, Evolution, and Intelligent Design*. Grand Rapids: Zondervan, 2017.
Suddendorf, Thomas, and David L. Butler. "The Nature of Visual Self-Recognition." *Trends in Cognitive Sciences* 17 (2013) 121–27.
Suddendorf, Thomas, and Janie Busby. "Mental Time Travel in Animals?" *Trends in Cognitive Sciences* 7 (2003) 391–96.
Suddendorf, Thomas, and Michael C. Corballis. "The Evolution of Foresight: What Is Mental Time Travel, and Is It Unique to Humans?" *Behavioral and Brain Sciences* 30 (2007) 299–313.
Swenson, Adam. "Intrinsic Value, Pain, and Method." In "Pain and Value," PhD diss., Rutgers University, 2006. http://www.csun.edu/~ars62917/Diss/Pain%20and%20value.html.
———. "Pain's Evils." *Utilitas* 21 (2009) 197–216.

Bibliography

Tulving, Endel. "Episodic Memory and Autonoesis: Uniquely Human?" In *The Missing Link in Cognition: Origins of Self-Reflective Consciousness*, edited by Herbert S. Terrace and Janet Metcalfe, 3–56. New York: Oxford University Press, 2005.

———. "Memory and Consciousness." *Canadian Psychology* 26 (1985) 1–12.

van Woudenberg, René. "A Brief History of Theodicy." In *The Blackwell Companion to the Problem of Evil*, edited by Justin P. McBrayer and Daniel Howard-Snyder, 177–91. Chichester: Wiley-Blackwell, 2013.

Ward, Keith. "The Evil-God Challenge—A Response." *Think* 14 (2015) 43–49.

Washburn, David A., et al. "Rhesus Monkeys (*Macaca mulatta*) Immediately Generalize the Uncertain Response." *Journal of Experimental Psychology: Animal Behavior Processes* 32 (2006) 185–89.

Weaver, Christopher Gregory. "Evilism, Moral Rationalism, and Reasons Internalism." *International Journal for Philosophy of Religion* 77 (2015) 3–24.

Wennberg, Robert. "Animal Suffering and the Problem of Evil." *Christian Scholar's Review* 21 (1991) 120–40.

Wheeler, Mark A., et al. "Toward a Theory of Episodic Memory: The Frontal Lobes and Autonoetic Consciousness." *Psychological Bulletin* 121 (1997) 331–54.

Wiertel, Derek Joseph. "Classical Theism and the Problem of Animal Suffering." *Theological Studies* 78 (2017) 659–95.

Wykstra, Stephen J. "The Humean Obstacle to Evidential Arguments from Suffering: On Avoiding the Evils of 'Appearance'." *International Journal for Philosophy of Religion* 16 (1984) 73–93.

Yancey, Philip, and Paul Brand. *The Gift of Pain*. Grand Rapids: Zondervan, 1997.

Zentall, Thomas R. "The Case for a Cognitive Approach to Animal Learning and Behavior." *Behavioural Processes* 54 (2001) 65–78.

Index

A

acts of the mind
  apprehension, 66, 68
  judgment, 66–67, 69, 81, 83
  reasoning, 65–72, 87
angels, 1, 16, 102
animal (nonhuman)
  awareness, 23–24, 30, 49, 61–62, 81–83, 87
  consciousness, 18–20, 23–24, 55, 60–65, 83, 88
  deification, 26–28
  episodic memory, 61, 68, 73, 77–81, 87
  metacognition, 61, 68, 72–77, 79–81, 83, 87
  mirror self-recognition, 72–73
  moral standing, 16, 27
  pain, 19–20, 23–25, 30–31, 36–37, 46–53, 58, 60–62, 80–90, 110
  proto-logic, 69–70
  self-awareness, 26, 32, 55, 61, 65, 68, 72–73, 77, 80–81, 83, 86–88, 110
  rationality, 15, 26, 32, 61, 64–66, 68–73, 76, 79–81, 87, 110
  resurrection, 26, 28, 30, 86
  theory of mind, 72–73
anxiety, 45, 52
Arango-Muñoz, Santiago, 76

argument
  animal deification, 26–28
  chaos-to-order, 24–25, 29–30
  nomic-regularity, 24, 29, 89
Aristotle, 2, 14–16, 54–55, 63, 65, 96
atheism, 11, 36–37
Augustine, 1–2, 15–17, 24, 136–37, 141
Avicenna, 65
Aquinas, Thomas
  on being, 54–55, 57, 93, 135–37, 139, 141–42
  on communicating God's goodness, 87, 92, 94–100, 129
  on God's goodness, 54–57, 93–94, 136–37
  on God's moral perfection, 55–57, 93–94, 104–5, 117–25, 131
  on God's purpose for creation, 94–95
  on God's sovereignty, 138
  on goodness, 54–55, 57, 93–95, 119–20, 128, 136–37, 142
  on hell, 124
  on moral evil, 38–39, 138–39
  on natural evil, 38–39, 85
  on necessity of a hierarchy of beings, 92, 96–100
  on pain, 39–42
  on reason, 65–66
  on self-knowledge, 67–68
  on suffering, 39–42, 85–87
  on the nature of evil, 38–39, 137–39

Index

B

Bermúdez, José, 69–70
best possible world, 96, 116, 119–20, 126, 130–31
Brand, Paul, 50–51

C

chaos-to-order argument—see argument, chaos-to-order
Christ, self-emptying of, 22
Collins, John, 134–36, 141–42
concupiscible emotion—see emotion, concupiscible
consciousness
    anoetic, 83–84
    autonoetic, 83
    noetic, 83–84
creationism
    evolutionary, 111
    old-earth, 111–13, 115
    progressive, 111
    young-earth, 32, 110–14
Creegan, Nicola Hoggard, 25–26, 29–31

D

Darwin, Charles, 3–6, 12–13
Davies, Brian, 56, 103, 121, 123
Dawkins, Richard, 4, 9–10
death
    before the Fall, 107, 113–15, 117, 125–31
    natural for corruptible beings, 105–8, 131, 139
deism, 22
depression, 39, 45–49, 84
Descartes, René, 17–20, 23, 62–63
design tradeoff, 53, 59, 88
despair, 41–42, 45–47
Dionysius—see Pseudo-Dionysius
Dougherty, Trent, 26–31
Draper, Paul, 4, 12–14, 88–91, 106–10
dual-process theory—see theory, dual-process
dual-system theory—see theory, dual-system
dualism, 17–19

E

emotion
    concupiscible, 40–41
    homeostatic, 43, 84
    irascible, 41–42
estimative power, 41, 65–66, 80
ethics
    consequentialist theory of, 104, 113, 115–21, 126, 128, 130–31
    deontological theory of, 113, 115–19, 126, 128, 130
    virtue theory of, 104, 115, 117, 123, 125
Evans, Jonathan St. B. T., 71–72
evil
    Darwinian problem of, 13, 90–92
    evidential problem of, 12, 31, 34–35, 59–60, 90
    gratuitous, 11, 34–36
    Humean problem of, 5–6, 50
    inference-to-the-best-explanation argument from, 90–91
    logical problem of, 11, 104
    moral, 1–2, 28, 38–39, 86, 138
    natural, 1–2, 24, 28, 38–39, 85–86, 112, 114, 126
    privation view of, 38–39, 46–50, 84–85, 105, 107, 134–37, 139–43
evil-god challenge, 133–36, 139, 143
evil-god hypothesis, 133–35

F

fear, 41–42, 44–48, 81, 84
Fiske, John, 4, 6–7
Five Ways, 54–55, 93, 125, 136, 139–40
Forrest, Peter, 134
Francescotti, Robert, 28–29, 37, 49–50, 82–84
free will, 1, 65, 85–86, 88, 96, 118, 120, 129, 138

Index

G

Garcia, Laura, 104, 115–17, 120, 123–24
Garrigou-Lagrange, Reginald, 95
God
    co-suffering of, 22
    desirability, 55, 57, 59, 103, 125, 137
    eternality, 119
    goodness, 7, 31, 36, 54–59, 87, 92–100, 102–11, 113–15, 117, 119, 122, 124–32
    hiddenness, 13
    infinity, 36, 55–57, 59, 104, 119, 137
    invisible, 56
    just, 27, 57–58, 86, 104–5, 121–25, 128–32, 137, 139
    loving, 26–27, 57–60, 87, 89, 100, 104–5, 110–11, 123–25, 128–30, 132, 137, 139–40
    moral perfection, 107, 113–23, 125, 128, 130–31
    omnipotence, 27, 51, 59–60, 89, 95, 103–4, 111, 113, 128, 131
    omniscience, 51, 99–100, 103, 113, 116, 128
    perfection, 55–56, 59, 92, 94–97, 100, 107, 116–17, 119–23, 126, 128–31, 137, 140
    purpose for creating, 94–95
    simplicity, 103, 121, 123, 125
    transcendence, 57, 103, 121, 143
good-god hypothesis, 133–34
goodness
    absence of, 38, 40, 48, 84, 137
    desirability of, 54–55, 93, 142
    metaphysical, 46–50, 58, 60, 86–88, 94, 104, 109, 119, 127
    negation of, 38
    privation of, 38–39, 42, 47, 105, 107, 138
    privation view of, 136, 140–43
Gray, Asa, 3

H

Haarsma, Deborah, 112
Ham, Ken, 112–13, 126
Harrison, Peter, 17, 20
Hendricks, Perry, 134
hierarchy of being, 16, 92, 96, 99–103, 105, 108–11, 129, 131
higher-order thought, 23–24, 30, 62, 80, 85, 87
Holyoak, Keith, 75
Hooker, Joseph, 4
hope, 41–42
Hull, David L., 4, 9
Hume, David, 4–5, 50
hunger, 43–44, 84

I

intellect, 15, 63, 65–68, 85–87, 99, 101–3, 123
    active, 67
    passive, 67
irascible emotion—see emotion, irascible
Irenaeus, 1

K

Kane, G. Stanley, 39, 42, 46
Kretzmann, Norman, 97

L

language
    analogical, 104
    univocal, 58, 135, 139
Law, Stephen, 133–36, 139–40, 143
laws
    eternal, 55, 104
    moral, 96, 104, 118–19
    natural, 55, 96, 101, 103, 110
    physical, 24, 53, 58–59, 87, 89, 96, 101, 118
Le Pelley, Mike, 74
leprosy, 50
Lewis, C. S., 19–20
logical problem of evil—see evil, logical problem of
logical problem of death before the Fall, 113–14, 125–30

Index

M

Mackie, J. L., 11, 104
Marchand, Serge, 46–47
memory
    episodic, 61, 68, 73, 77–81, 87
    semantic, 77–79
mental time-travel, 78–79
metacognition, 72–77, 79–81, 83, 87
    anoetic, 76, 81
    autonoetic, 76, 80–81
    noetic, 76, 81
    self-attributive, 73, 76–77, 80–81
    self-evaluative, 73–74, 76
Metcalfe, Janet, 76
moral evil—see evil, moral
More, Henry, 19
Murray, Michael, 23–25, 28–31, 37, 49–50, 61, 82

N

natural evil—see evil, natural
naturalism, 13, 32, 89–92, 101, 107–10
neo-Cartesianism, 19–20, 23–24, 28–30, 49, 60–65, 80, 82–83, 88–89
neo-Darwinianism, 20
neo-Thomism, 61, 80, 82–83, 86, 88
nociception—see pain, nociception
no-design hypothesis, 13, 90–91, 107–10
nomic-regularity argument—see argument, nomic-regularity

P

pain
    chronic, 51–52
    nociception, 43, 46
    sensation of, 43–44, 48, 84
    unpleasantness of, 43–44, 48, 50–51, 85, 88–89
Penn, Derek, 75
Povinelli, Daniel, 75
privation, evil as—see evil, privation view of
privation, good as—see goodness, privation view of
problem of no best world, 116
Proust, Joëlle, 73
Pseudo-Dionysius, 95, 129, 137

R

reasoning
    abstract, 66–72, 81, 87
    discursive, 67
religious language—see language
Rescorla, Michael, 70
Robson, Mark, 39, 42, 46
Ross, Glenn, 22–24, 61
Ross, Hugh, 112
Rowe, William L., 4, 11–12, 14, 31–32, 34–37, 50–54, 58–61, 80–81, 88–89, 110–11
Russell, Bertrand, 4, 7–8
Ryken, Philip, 114, 126

S

sadness, 44–45, 47–48, 84
Satan, 30
Scrutton, Anastasia, 134
self-awareness, 26, 32, 55, 61, 65, 68, 72–81, 83, 86–88, 110
Shanley, Brian, 121
Smith, David, 74
Smith, Quentin, 4, 8
Son, Lisa, 76
sorrow, 40–42, 44, 47, 81
soul
    rational, 2, 14–16, 32, 63–64, 86–87
    sensitive, 14–15, 63–64, 87
    vegetative, 14–15, 64
Southgate, Christopher, 20–22, 25, 30–31
Stanovich, Keith, 72

Index

suffering
    as natural for corruptible beings, 47–50, 84–86, 105–7, 110
    as privation of the willed good, 85–87
    nature of animal, 34–53
    pointless—see evil, gratuitous
Swenson, Adam, 48
symmetry thesis, 133–36, 139, 142

T

theism
    Christian, 13–14, 91–92, 106, 108–10
    classical, 31–32, 58, 89, 111, 113–14, 133–35, 139, 143
    skeptical, 35, 58, 134, 139
theodicy
    evil-as-privation, 135–43
    evolutionary, 21
    free will, 133
    reverse, 133, 135, 140–43
    semantic, 134–36, 139–41, 143
    soul-making, 2, 26–28, 30, 133
    Thomistic, 139–43
theory
    dual-process, 71–72, 76
    dual-system, 70–71
    evolutionary, 6, 9, 13, 25–26, 90, 107–10
    natural selection, 3, 5, 13, 22, 90

thirst, 43–44, 84
Transcendental Argument for Animal Deification—see argument, animal deification
Tulving, Endel, 78–79, 82–83

V

virtues
    art, 56, 122, 137
    chastity, 56, 59, 123
    fortitude, 28, 56, 59, 117
    justice, 56, 59, 104, 117, 137
    liberality, 56, 59, 122, 137, 140
    love, 56, 104, 122–23, 125
    magnificence, 56, 122, 137
    mercy, 122–23, 128, 130–32
    prudence, 104, 117, 122, 137
    sobriety, 56, 59, 123
    temperance, 117, 123
    truth, 56, 59, 104, 122, 137

W

Ward, Keith, 134
Weaver, Christopher, 134
will, 1, 15, 38–39, 56, 58, 60, 63, 65, 85–86, 88, 90, 94–96, 100, 103–7, 118–22, 124, 128–29, 131, 138–43
Wykstra, Stephen, 35